Heal Your Inner Child

Learn the Art of Re-parenting, Break the Chain of Generational Patterns, Discover Your Natural Talents, and Unleash Your Limitless Potential.

Tina Ashok Dhingra

Acknowledgment

Thanks to my grandmother for giving good values to our family. Thanks to my father and mother for all the love and care, giving me good education. Thanks to my husband, Sanju, for giving me valuable feedback on my book. I have been blessed with some wonderful mentors in my life. Thank you Joy sir, Amol sir, and Som sir for your guidance. Thanks to my friend Akhil for pushing me to complete this book. My Cute Pet IVA, thanks. Thanks to myself for taking consistent actions and not giving up.

Table of Contents

1. A Journey from Pure Soul to Wounded Soul

"One person's trauma is another's loss of innocence." ~Jodi Picoult

What happens to the beautiful beginning when we were all born as pure souls?

The soul has seven innate qualities inherited from the supreme soul (God). Purity, Peace, Love, Joy, Bliss, Powers, and Knowledge.

Do you know why people change the true nature of the soul?

How do some pure souls become murderers, drug addicts, physical and sexual offenders, cruel dictators, morally degenerate politicians, etc.?

How do they become the "walking wounded" and harm others?

A soul that can do wonders and more incredible things is now converted into anger, greed, jealousy, sloth, and vengeance?

We see all around us the sad, fearful, doubting, anxious, and depressed, and those filled with unutterable longings. Indeed, this loss of our innate human potential is the greatest tragedy.

We can even prevent this from happening to our children in the future.

The more we learn about how we lost our true selves and go deep into our childhood and find the stories that made us like this is the first step in a healing journey. The more we understand the patterns and take responsibility to work on our emotional wounds, the more we will find ways to return to our true nature.

2. Uncovering My Deep Rooted Emotions

"You have to dig deep within yourself in order to find your best self, some people aren't willing to do this, and this is why mediocrity exists." ~Royale Lradin

It was 2019. I was at my in-law's house, Gwalior, in MP (India). We planned to attend a wedding. I had a beautiful dress and wanted to wear that dress to the wedding. But my husband told me to wear a red saree, which I did not want to wear.

I told him again that I wanted to wear this dress, not the one you want me to wear. But he said no, wear this one only; it is better. I started feeling irritated and suffocated. I felt uncomfortable like someone was trying to suppress me. I started crying and shouting at my husband. My whole body was vibrating with anger.

With anger, I asked him:

- Did I ask your opinion on what I should wear or not?
- Can I decide for myself?
- Why should I wear what you like?

My anger was so intense that I felt like throwing things at him. I had to drink water to relax. After some time, I realized what was wrong with me. Why did I behave like that? I could say politely that I wanted to wear this and not that. I started reflecting. The way I behaved was not usual. The sensations of emotions I felt in my body had so much intensity.

Where was this anger coming from? I started writing a journal about my anger. Whenever I used to get angry, I would write the date and about the incident in detail.

Why did this happen? How much was the intensity?

I started digging and tried to find the root cause of my anger. Why did I feel so much anger for this particular issue? I tried to remember my childhood incidents related to it.

Do you know what I found?

When I was around ten years old, I used to wear boy's clothes. One day I went to someone's house wearing a kurta pyjama (a traditional Indian dress for men), and one aunty asked me, whose son are you?

I was a flat-chested thin girl. My walking style was like a boy. It was as if I had a boy's soul but in a girl's body. Why did I wear boy's clothes of all types? One logical reason I could deduce was that I used to get my older brother's old clothes.

Another reason is one I have never understood until today. The new clothes my mother used to buy for me were boy's clothes. Maybe it was because I had a younger brother, and the clothes could have been passed on to him in the future.

I am still thinking about it, trying to figure it out.

My elder brother and I used to wear the same type of t-shirts, only the colors differed. The same thing used to happen with my school dress: instead of wearing a skirt and shirt, I used to wear a shirt and pants as a school dress. I would get an old one from my older brother.

My entire identity was almost like a boy - from my walking style, clothes, looks, and haircut. I also became conditioned that it was OK to wear boy clothes. I never asked anything and never questioned it. I was a timid, less expressive, and non-demanding kind of girl.

I used to think that was a regular thing. But deep down, I missed wearing beautiful fairy frocks and girly dresses. I clearly remember it was my birthday; at that time, there were no smartphones, mobile photos, or social media trends.

So, if we needed to take a photo, we used to go to the photo studio to get it taken. There was a new tradition of taking pictures on birthdays. That's why I wanted to get my photograph taken on my birthday too.

But when I opened my Almira, I found nothing that I loved. This was the first time I realized that I didn't have girly clothes. And then I wanted to change my identity.

I cried for the fairy frocks. My mother told me that one of my cousins had a beautiful dress and asked to borrow her frock for the photograph. I felt a lot of hesitation to ask anything from anyone because of my super shy nature.

I asked my mother, can you please ask her. Mother said no, I will not ask. She said, if you want to wear it, you should ask. I was hesitant as I was scared of my aunt, my cousin's mother.

I kept trying to convince my mother, but she said, "you give your clothes to her to wear sometimes, so why can't you ask?" I said, I don't know, mom, but I don't dare ask.

Wearing a fairy frock and getting the picture taken was a desire so intense that I finally prepared and pushed myself to ask. I asked my cousin, and she asked her mother. Her mother opened the storage trunk of their old bed as in those days, we used to keep clothes in a bed storage.

As a reward for pushing myself, I got a beautiful white and red frock. My cousin placed it in my hands, and I was thrilled to see it.

I wore it, but on my feet, I did not have beautiful footwear, so I wore my black belly shoes, the ones I used to wear to school.

I also wanted to decorate my hair like a princess. I looked at myself in the mirror, saw short hair, and felt really sad. I decided to buy a pink hairband and put it in my hair. then I went with my cousin to the photographer's shop.

*(Whenever I see this picture, I remember all the emotions.
I know that is why I was not smiling in the picture.)*

Everything around you and within you explains
existence; dig deep, explore everything, and you'll find
the answers you seek.

3. Unlocking the Secrets of the Subconscious Mind

"Who is controlling your life.... Not you, really. It's your subconscious mind, a power within you." ~Fastlane Freedom

Our conscious mind is only 5% responsible for our activities, including logical thinking, short-term memory, willpower, and critical thinking. Then, who is responsible for 95% of the decisions in our life?

Who is hidden under the surface or behind the curtains, someone we cannot see, taking charge of our life and running the show while we are unaware of it?

Our subconscious mind is responsible for 95% of our decisions.

Our subconscious mind is many times more powerful than the conscious mind.

The subconscious mind takes care of the body's essential, everyday operations, such as breathing, sleeping, and keeping organs functioning. It is also responsible for repressing feelings, suppressing memories, and controlling the habits, thoughts, desires, and reactions that may be hurtful, awkward, and shameful.

The subconscious can be considered a vast memory bank, storing our experiences, emotions, and beliefs. Just like a computer, it has an almost limitless capacity for retaining data.

An example of low self-esteem is when every compliment sounds sarcastic

Having an internal belief of not looking good. If someone tells you, "you are so beautiful," it seems like a cruel prank. Such a thought is likely due to the long-held belief that you are not attractive.

Your subconscious acts like a detective, investigating the countless programs of your mind to identify any experiences of rejection. Choosing to pursue ambitions and creating something unique in life can be difficult if negative patterns, tales, and emotional traumas are not addressed.

"The power of our subconscious is beyond our measure."

4. The Unspoken War Within: My Story of Self-Hatred

"There are wounds that never show on the body that are deeper and more hurtful than anything that bleeds." ~Laurell K Hamilton

I remember going to multiple marriages wearing a pant-shirt. One marriage om my mother's side of the family was my mother's cousin.

What was I wearing? It was a shirt and pants, both made of the same dark purple color fabric. There was a front zip instead of buttons on the shirt, and there were all sorts of animals printed on it, a lion, giraffe, monkey, etc. It was like a zoo scene on the front and back, and thank God the pant was plain, not printed.

Under that shirt, I wore a white color t-shirt. This is what I could do to enhance my style so I could open the zipper and show my white t-shirt, which was soothing and simple.

I saw girls in sparkling skirts, bangles, Bindi, long hair, and beautiful necklaces. They looked so beautiful with open hair and makeup. I felt so broken inside.

I watched them repeatedly because they looked so beautiful and attractive. In the other hand, I was boy in appearance, wearing boy's clothes with no earrings nor necklace. I had to wear that zoo theme pants and shirt set, looking like Mowgli's brother from the "Jungle book."

I remember my mother introducing me to her cousin, telling him, "She is my daughter."

I was like, "Oh really"? "Your daughter?"

"Are you sure I am a girl?" Do I look like a girl from any angle? Even I was not sure if I was a girl or a boy from my looks.

I can still hear the loud music when everyone was dancing on the floor. the hall was filled with lots of relatives; everyone was meeting and greeting each other, but I was very lonely.

 I didn't want to meet anyone. I didn't want to show my face, what I was wearing, or how I looked/ I just wanted to hide and stay hidden.

I started feeling suffocated and irritated. After seeing other girls laughing and giggling, I started feeling unimportant and invisible. Tears started rolling down my cheeks even though I tried hard to hide them. I could not stop my tears anymore, so I ran into a room where a few old people were resting.

I watched myself in the mirror, displaying so much anger. I could not stop crying. In fact, I started crying even more and said to myself, "How bad you look, Tina. My eyes and my face had become red.

Near the mirror, I saw a face cream from a famous brand, "Fair and Lovely." I applied it to my face to hide my tears and look fresh so I could go back. Even though I used the cream to prepare myself, I broke down again and started crying heavily.

I applied the cream again but could not overcome that feeling. I hated myself at that moment. I was crying a lot, thinking about how bad I looked. Why can't I look like them?

Beautiful!

Hating yourself is the worst. When others hate you, at least you can go home and relax. When you hate yourself, there is no escape.

I went to plenty of weddings like this - in a shirt and pants. I wore a t-shirt and jeans in the summers while in winter, I wore my brother's coat and pants.

I wore a dark sky-blue coat and pants to a marriage. Can you imagine a little girl wearing a shirt, coat, and pants, and boy's hair cut?

I don't know why I could not express my feelings, and why I could not ask. I could not say firmly that this is what I don't like, or this is what I want. I was so suppressed. I did not have any voice.

5. Understanding Inner Child Healing and Emotional Wounds

"The inner child is a part of our personality that stores all our memories, feelings, needs, reactions, attitude towards ourselves and others, and behaviours that we have preserved from our childhood." ~Katya Ki

An inner child is the child within us and has been there since we were conceived. The unconscious part of our mind holds our childhood's good or bad memories and experiences.

When in childhood, our most profound needs of love, recognition, praise, attention, protection, and other types of emotional support go unmet, the void of the unfulfilled desires of our inner child become emotional wounds after being hurt on an emotional or psychological level.

In the English dictionary, **"wound"** refers to an injury to the body, such as skin or flesh cuts or tears. It goes on to say that a wound is also an injury to a person's reputation or feelings. This definition covers both physical and emotional wounds.

A physical wound from a physical point of view, generally refers to living tissue that has been damaged. The damage could be internal or external, visible to an eye or through X-rays. One good thing about a physical wound is that one can see if the injury is big or small and whether it's bleeding, infected, or healing.

On the other hand, an **emotional wound** is an uncomfortable or unpleasant experience that causes deep mental and psychological pain. This pain goes on and on, lasting weeks, months, or even years.

Some wounds are physical while others are emotional or psychological. In some instances, a person may suffer from both types of injuries. What is expected in all situations is pain.

Every individual in pain desires to receive healing, whether physical or emotional.

Healing is getting well again, especially after a cut or other wounds. Most wounding experiences happen unexpectedly, and when it happens, we were meek or not strong enough to raise our voices, protect, or defend ourselves.

We assume that all will heal with time, but the reality is that emotional scars become even more significant and compounded if we don't cure them in the first place. They are like physical wounds; if you do not treat them at the right time, the infection will spread throughout the whole body.

"Emotional wounds are even more dangerous than physical wounds."

For example, if someone's hand is broken and covered with a plaster cast, you can see it. Because you can see it, you feel sympathy for that person. Everyone understands that if someone is not physically fit, you get care and compassion from others, but emotional scars are so profound that no one can see them. Even at a job or in school, you get leave (sick leave) if you are not physically fit. Now, what about the emotional scars where you can't see blood, fractures, or any kind of injury? People just can't see it. They do not care until someone really shares.

The problem is that most people don't want to share their emotional scars because they are attached to their fears, guilt, anger, hate, which no one generally wants to discuss.

6. Discovered the Incredible Power of Mirror Work!

"You must be fearless enough to give yourself the love you did not receive." ~Oprah Winfrey

While growing up, I had issues with my self-esteem as I did not like myself. I failed to find love within and instead looked for it from others. My understanding of love was that we love others, and others love us back in return.

Unfortunately, this didn't work for me, and I was feeling broken and hurt after each failed relationship with friends, family, and a partner.

When I learned about the concept of self-love, my life changed. I started doing mirror work.

Mirror work is an exercise where we look at the mirror, see ourselves, and repeat positive affirmations such as "I love myself" and "I am so beautiful."

I started saying these affirmations and doing everything for myself, no matter what I was expecting from others. Gradually I was filled with a lot of self-love with no expectations from others. Whatever love to me came from others was a bonus.

My journey of self-hatred began with a mirror in my childhood. I hated myself in a marriage, where I looked in the mirror, cried, and said, "Tina, you are not beautiful." But as I started practicing self-love with the mirror and kept telling myself that I am beautiful, doors of love opened.

Mirror work worked like magic in my healing journey. **_I converted my mirror-work journey into a poem._**

The Power of Mirror Work

The power of mirror work, it's something worth sharing,

It's something to practice. It's daring.

The concept of mirror work was so new to me,

But I listened, and with courage, I did see.

My eyes met my reflection. I was scared of what I'd see

But then I decided to look closer and accept me.

I looked at the mirror and said slowly,

Tina, I am here.

I said it first with a bit of fear,

Not knowing if I could even hear,

The tears started rolling down my face,

My childhood was full of self-hate and disgrace,

The mirror was the source of my childhood pain,

And it was the source of my jealousy and shame.

But healing started when I looked in the mirror.

It felt strange at first, but the feelings grew strong

Now I'd look in the mirror, and it would be a song

And the words came out with strength and grace,

"I love you, Tina. You are beautiful in every place."

Seeing myself in the mirror, I started to cry,

But the tears weren't of sadness, but of joy.

The old beliefs of beauty slowly disappeared,

And a new impression of beauty slowly appeared.

It changed my life so much better than before.

It made me happy. It made me explore

The love I feel for myself each day,

Is a gift that will never go away,

So if ever you're feeling unsure and down,

I wish you look in the mirror and smile, not frown.

I started loving myself,
and my relationships improved,

I started sending out love,
and I started receiving love too.

The love I received now felt different.

It is a love that comes from within.

7. How Our Emotional Wounds Affect Our Quality of Life

"When our inner child is not nurtured and nourished, our minds gradually close to new ideas, unprofitable commitments and the surprises of the spirit." ~Brennan Manning

1) Taking wrong decisions- our decision-making at a subconscious level reflects our inner child as it is part of our beliefs about ourselves. Our quality of life depends upon the decisions we make.

We make wrong decisions based on bad experiences when emotionally hurt or wounded. Imagine you are choosing the wrong job, wrong friends, wrong career, wrong life partner, wrong city, and wrong hobbies because of past emotional trauma.

Think about how will your quality of life be.

2) Generational patterns-If you don't heal, you will pass on your emotional traumas to your kids. We not only pass our house, property, jewelry, furniture, and money to the next generation, but we also pass physical and emotional health through our genes. We have seen many it times: doctors check our backgrounds before selecting a treatment, and these days, even the "to-be spouse" has similar questions because we also inherit issues from our parents, grandparents, etc.

Doctors generally ask these questions:

- *Does anybody in your family have this disease?*

- *Does any of your mother or father have this disease?*

Now my question to you is: why do doctors ask these questions? To know if the disease is genetic or not since you will transfer all your emotional baggage to your kids.

3) You can hurt others: if you do not heal yourself, you will continue hurting others. This pain chain will continue until you don't break it.

4) Dreams and goals: How can you see goals and dreams clearly with those painful eyes? When you are in emotional pain, you can't see a brighter future, and you will miss a fantastic opportunity because you cannot see it with painful eyes. Though everything will remain the same, your perspective can change things entirely.

Life is like a journey. Imagine you are traveling somewhere with a heavy bag on your shoulders. Can you go the extra mile?

Maybe you reach somewhere, and then you feel tired and exhausted, unable to enjoy yourself when you get to your goal. We sometimes think while traveling, I wish I had not taken this big bag with me? Then my journey would have been much easier, faster, and more comfortable.

The emotional bags you carry from the past also make you mentally and emotionally tired, slowing your progress.

So, heal yourself and remove your emotional baggage.

8. Embracing My Unfulfilled Desires

"Your wound is probably not your fault, but your healing is your responsibility." ~Denice Frohman

I had two choices: feeling sad about my past or taking responsibility to nurture my inner child. I knew my inner child wanted to wear some dresses, so I asked myself and made a list of them that my inner child wanted to wear. I promised myself I would take care of all my unfulfilled desires. I became the parent of my inner child.

These were the three things that my inner child wanted to wear.

- Long black leather boots
- Fairy gown to look like a princess
- A shimmery black dress with slit to show my legs.

- I felt very confident when I wore long black boots.
- I can't explain my happiness or how I felt when I wore a beautiful gown.
- I felt much more feminine wearing a black dress with a front slit.

9. Benefits of Healing Your Inner Child

"We nurture our creativity when we release our inner child. Let it run and roam free. It will take you on a brighter journey." ~Serina Hartwell

- Understanding how past trauma affects our present behavior and the healing of our inner child, we create the safety and security our younger selves have always needed.
- Doing so increases self-esteem, self-compassion, and compassion for others.
- We unlock our natural gifts, inner curiosity, and limitless capacity to love ourselves and others.
- We reconnect to our passions, dreams, and talents, which we may have put aside. We feel empowered and in control of our lives. Finally! We return back to the true nature of our soul.

10. Three Steps of the Healing Process

(Awareness>Acceptance>Action)

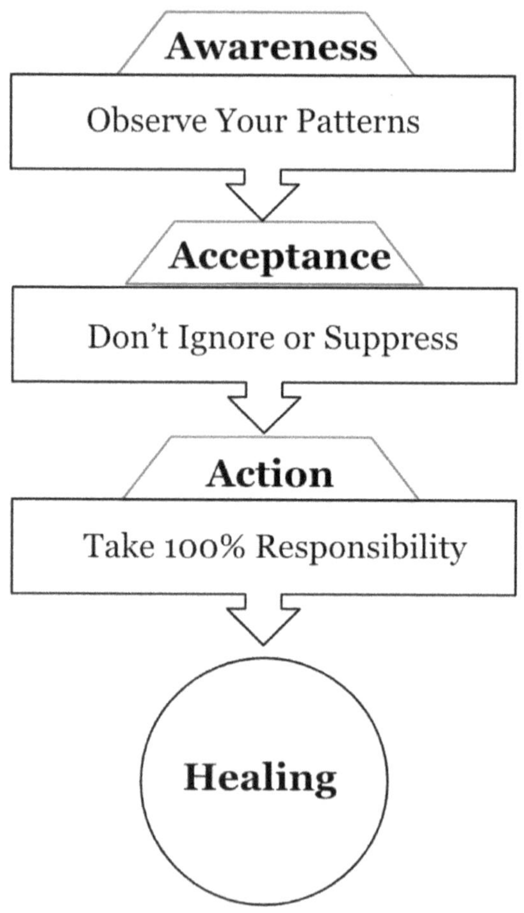

Part 1: AWARENESS

11. Know Your Wounded Inner Child

"Until you make the unconscious conscious, it will direct your life and you will call it fate." -Carl Jung

We can only gain proper awareness once we stop blaming the situation, the people, and the place for our suffering. Awareness comes from observing something deeply. When we look at our problems from a bird's eye view, we observe our repetitive patterns and try to connect the dots.

We get clarity when our self-created bubbles of unrealistic experiences burst and we enter the real world. Then we start realizing how wrong our thinking process was; while growing up, we often had this feeling in life whenever our bubble bursts.

Awareness brings growth and wisdom into our lives.

I am sure you must have burst many bubbles of misconceptions yourself. We look inside and are ready to take responsibility for ourselves instead of blaming the whole world.

Your wounded inner child is always there, craving attention. We don't know or don't have awareness, but it does not mean it's not there.

Awareness comes from observations, and observation comes from repetitive patterns.

Beneath the ocean's surface is stillness, and underneath there are hidden currents. All our truths are hidden deep down in our ocean subconsciousness.

My suggestions:

Try to do meditation for at least 15 minutes morning or evening, or practice 15 minutes of silence in a day.

Try to write a journal daily and cover all the issues in detail. You will be ready with lots of data and examples.

While doing meditation, try to write if you get some clarity; otherwise, later, you will not be able to recall your thoughts. Keeping a journal really helped me find my own patterns.

Find a natural or calm place, sit with your journal, and try to reflect on all the issues. List some pointers and try to find patterns.

Doing this diligently will surprise you as it will reveal many interesting facts about yourself. If you can open yourself up to newer experiences, you can achieve real awareness. You will sense that some layer or shields were removed from your eyes, and you have entered the real world. You will understand the real reasons behind all the drama.

The day you will understand how badly your inner child wants you to visit him/her.

That day you will gain awareness about your inner child for the first time.

12. Signs and Symptoms of a Wounded Inner Child

"So many broken children living in grown bodies mimicking adult lives." -Ijeoma Umebinyuo

Are you experiencing frustration or feeling blocked in some area of your life? Give your inner child the attention it needs. This could involve trouble at work or with parenting, finding or sustaining love, building relationships, or defining your limits.

1) Abandonment wound: The individual may feel "left out" and fear being alone, hating the feeling of loneliness. They may become co-dependent, threatening to leave if not given sufficient attention, usually attracting emotionally unavailable people.

2) Guilt wound: I feel "sorry" or "bad" because I don't like to ask for things. I often regret my actions when I don't speak for myself. I use guilt to influence people and find it hard to set firm boundaries. As a result, I often find myself surrounded by people who make me feel guilty.

3) Trust wound- Fear of being hurt, a lack of self-trust, and searching for methods to not rely on others. Feeling uncertain, needing excessive external approval, and feeling unsafe. As a result, they usually attract people who also feel unsafe.

4) Neglect wound- Having difficulty releasing emotions, a lack of self-confidence while being prone to outbursts of anger, unable to turn down requests, keeping feelings inside, and worrying about being exposed. Attracts typically people who don't appreciate them or make them feel "seen."

If someone has many bad experiences, he/she may have more than 1 or 2 wounds.

13. Why My Inner Child Was Hurt

Inner child work helps us get to the root of the problem- the core wounding – instead of putting a band-aid over the pain and hoping it gets better. ~Robert Jackman

I remember I was eight years old. On a cold winter day, I saw my elder brother drinking syrup. He did so every day. My parents always brought a new supply before the old one was finished. He kept taking it for many months. In the beginning, I paid little attention. I always saw empty and sometimes filled bottles in our kitchen.

After a few years, I learned that Ayurvedic syrup "Shankha-Pushpi" was to boost memory power, and my brother has been taking it for 2-3 years. After knowing this fact, I felt hurt and wondered why it was not given to me.

It wasn't like my parents hid it from me, but why had they not given it to me like they used to give it my older brother? Did I not have a brain? Or was there no need to boost my memory?

I remember crying and asking why they were not giving it to me. They started laughing when saying no. I was mad at my parents. I remember also starting to drink it. I still remember the green color of the syrup, the sweet taste, and the fact that we used to add the same ratio of water and syrup and mix it before drinking. But still, deep inside, my inner child was hurt by not giving me the same importance as my brother.

Interestingly, growing up, I got much better scores than my older brother. I used to say sarcastically, ***"what happened to that memory booster you drank in childhood? It didn't work out for you.***

I still crack this joke at him and laugh a lot.

When I started my inner work journey, I started writing everything - whatever hurt my inner child. I wrote about this incident. Although my parents gave me a good education and loved me so much, this was the one thing that my inner child did not like. When I realized it, I went with my husband to a store. I was not sure whether I would get this syrup or not because it was around a twenty-year-old thing. But the ayurvedic brand, Baidyanath, still had this product.

I bought it and asked my husband to take the picture. I was happy that day. The picture was to send to my older brother, the same one I am sharing with all of you.

I remember my brother's reply. He sent lots of laughing emojis and wrote back, "Ha ha, still you remember this syrup? I beamed a big smile at his reply and thought, maybe I forgot, but my inner child still remembers the pain of feeling hurt.

14. Different Archetypes of the Inner Child

"In my soul, I am still that small child who did not care about anything else but the beautiful colors of a rainbow.~ Papiya Ghosh

The inner child can be hurt through many means and ways, which may be overlooked or taken lightly. This hurt can come from neglect, mistreatment, and traumas encountered during childhood. On a spiritual level, forgiveness can be a way to heal the wounded child.

Child archetypes broadly can be divided into 5 types.

Type #1: The Orphaned Child

Children who feel unwanted and left out may have experienced something in the past that left them feeling insignificant or unimportant. This can even occur before birth, while in the mother's womb. Orphaned children often learn to become independent early, creating a disconnect with family. These children commonly have trust issues, struggle to socialize, and maintain distance from others.

Type #2: Magical Child

These types of children are highly creative or gifted. They often feel that anything is possible and achievable. They have a world of their own, full of vibrant dreams, fantasies, and magic. Despite dreaming big, they have great understanding of how different elements can come together. They trust the universe, allowing them to manifest their dreams more quickly.

These kids get wounded when people ridicule them by calling their dreams nonsense and childish. They often develop depression and lose their magical touch as they lose faith in themselves to achieve what they can dream of.

Magical children may develop depression when their belief in miracles is lost, mainly when they doubt their abilities. It is essential to encourage these youngsters to keep believing in the miraculous, so they can manifest their ambitions and continue to make their dreams come true.

Type #3: The Nature Child

These children have a strong affinity for the outdoors and are highly imaginative. They are in tune with the natural world and can sense the changing seasons. The energy of the environment. the life force that surrounds them. Nature children often collect shells, rocks, leaves, feathers, and more. They have a keen sensitivity and resilience, like nature itself.

When they witness people mistreating nature or animal life, the nature child gets hurt. They may become frustrated and isolated without sufficient opportunities to connect with nature.

Type #4: The Eternal Child

This type of person is full of energy and maintains youthful energy throughout life. They carry a sense of innocence and freedom and find joy in the little things.

The wounded child of this type resists taking responsibility for themselves or others. They may not like living by societal norms and live outside the standard structure of the adult world. They prefer to stay in a more carefree state of being. Unfortunately, this can lead to a feeling of being stuck in an earlier stage of life and lacking maturity, causing difficulty when trying to function in the adult world.

Type #5: The Needy Child

Like the "orphaned child," the needy child also got wounded through neglect, feeling left out, and not receiving what they deserve. They think no one loves, cares, or understands them.

They feel they should be getting more, yet they need to know precisely what that is. They never feel fulfilled and satisfied. They continually feel an emptiness in their life, constantly searching for something to fill the void and striving to reach the unknown.

The wounded inner child of this type often suffers depression, low self-esteem, and feels unimportant. This can lead to being unkind to others, as they are focused on meeting their needs and desires.

Type #6: The Divine Child:

The Divine child types can connect at a soul level and have a divine aura around them. They are pure, innocent, and gentle beings who vibrate at a higher energy level than others around them. They are very kind and compassionate by nature.

The hurt version of this child archetype turns into hypocrites who take advantage of their spiritual/religious power to trick people yet still present themselves as the loyal messenger of God and excellent human being.

If you notice any of the above types of wounded child, it's a red flag that it's time for you to heal your child. It indicates that your inner child is calling for your help, support, and attention. Now, it's your responsibility to reparent your inner child.

Many therapists have shared that the symptoms of a wounded inner child are standard, unfortunately, and can be identified easily. You may be experiencing these patterns as a result of childhood experiences. It's important to acknowledge how your inner child may feel and take steps toward providing it with the support and understanding it needs.

By addressing your childhood wounds and their effects on your adult life, you can begin to resolve and break free from these patterns. You first start by becoming more aware of this. Now that you have the opportunity, you should use it positively. Through this journey, you will have the chance to meet, heal, and help your wounded inner child and eventually break free from the fear that has plagued you for so long.

15. Case studies- Stories of Wounded Inner Child

" The most sophisticated people I've ever known had one thing in common: they were all in touch with the inner children."~ Jim Henson

Case Study#1: The journey of an inner child begins in the mother's womb.

Issues: Mary (changed name) had anger, jealousy, and self-worth issues. She always felt unimportant. When Mary was in her mother's womb, everyone was expecting a boy because the family already had a first girl child

Can you imagine the expectations and stress her mother went through while pregnant. Her mother was not strong enough to raise her voice to tell her in-laws that she didn't have the power to choose or alter the gender of the baby as per wish.

Influenced by peer pressure, her mother began to hope and pray for a baby boy. Everyone knows babies in utero can hear and sense feelings and emotions and even learn things.

Marry was in her mother's womb and felt the emotions of unwantedness, fear, and oppression. Can you imagine the family's environment, energy, and response when Marry was born? Was her mother joyful when she took her new born in her arms for the first time?

We think we don't remember all this because we were little; but subconsciously, we store all the memories and experiences from the time we are conceived. Traumas and their effects can persist into adulthood.

Sometimes we think, why I am like this or like that? or why someone behaves weirdly. We don't realize that our current behavior results from our past experiences.

Case Study #2:

Issues: John (changed name) always feared higher authority in his office. He always needed the courage to talk to management people in his office.

It all started when John was eight years old. His father's friend used to come home for a party. He was always told not to enter the room when they were smoking, drinking, and chatting. All of his father's friends were sitting in the drawing room. One day when he entered the room, his father scolded him badly. After that day, he feared going in front of them.

While growing up, John developed the habit of not talking to elderly people much and being quiet around them. When he started his first job, he noticed his body trembling and his hands shaking when he had to meet with senior management. He was confused about why this was happening until he uncovered the root cause - the events of his childhood.

Whenever you experience intense emotions, take a step back and try to look at the situation on a deeper level. Reflect on any childhood memories that could be associated with the incident.

Case Study - 3

Issues: Alisa (name changed) always had trust issues and relationship issues with her husband. When Alisa was in college, she was dating a guy named Ron (name changed). Alisa had genuine feelings for Ron. One day, he invited her to a party and attempted to pressure her into physical intimacy, which she wasn't emotionally prepared for. This left her feeling disheartened, and she ran out of the party, her trust in Ron broken.

After breaking up with Ron, she could not develop friendships with boys, believing they would all end similarly. This caused her to become bitter and wary of all boys, keeping her distance from them.

Alisa married Abel (name changed), a man her parents had found for her. Due to past experiences, she had grown to see physical intimacy as bad and felt immense emotional distress, believing her husband did not love her and was only with her for sex.

They had lots of fights because of the different expectations in their relationship. Abel needed to understand what the issues with Alisa were.

In every house, countless true stories result from our past experiences. If our emotional wounds remain unhealed, they will grow and accumulate and become more severe over time.

The 20s -30s is a time when the emotions that have been hidden and hurtful become more powerful and vibrant. Thinking about getting married while carrying these traumas can make married life very challenging.

Your partner may also have a wounded inner child.

Visualizing the worst-case scenario where both partners have unaddressed inner child issues, it becomes clear how difficult it can be for two emotionally wounded people to get along. The lack of understanding of why fights are occurring and where the anger is coming from can lead to divorce, as these two individuals may no longer be able to tolerate each other. Despite their love for each other, it may not be enough to keep them together.

Everyone looks at the surface level and understands the reaction, but none understands what is going on deep down. What are the person's unmet basic needs, or what has that person experienced in childhood compounded over the years?

If we do not take steps to heal from our trauma and continue to live with our partner in an average lifestyle, we may pass down our traumas to future generations.

Untreated emotional wounds can have far-reaching effects on our physical, mental, emotional, and spiritual well-being. These wounds can disturb our relationships, create obstacles in our job, and leave us without a clear sense of life's purpose and direction, ultimately resulting in a destroyed life.

Each person will have their own stories of difficulties they endured throughout childhood, so each journey is unique and one of self-discovery

16. The Drama Triangle

Drama does not just walk into your life either you create it, invite it or associate with it meaning. - Unknown

Stephen Karpman first described the Drama Triangle in the 1960s. It is a model representing a power game involving three roles: victim, rescuer, and persecutor, and each part represents a common and ineffective response to conflict.

Although all three are "roles" and none may be true to who we are, we can all get caught up in a hard-to-escape cycle. Most of us have neurological programming embedded deep in our brains that causes us to adopt one of three distinct roles depending on the context. We often find ourselves naturally taking one of these positions regardless of whether we are aware of it or not.

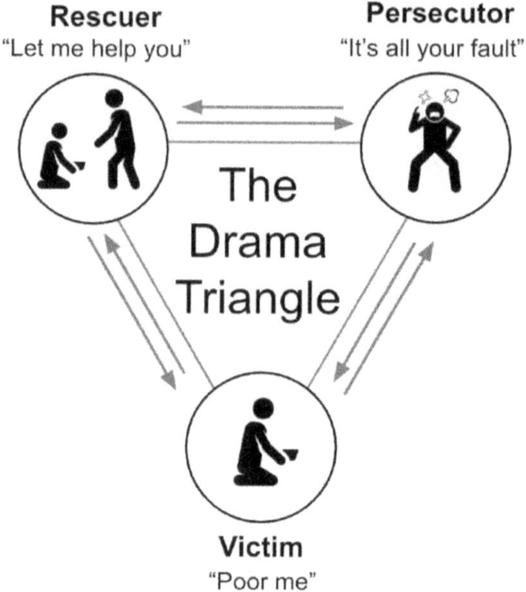

1)Victim – "Poor me"

(Victims don't take self-responsibility)

Victims feel helpless, hopeless, and trapped, seeing life as something that happens to them, unable to alter their circumstances. They also have an interest in confirming that their issue is unsolvable. These people view themselves as incapable and blame Persecutors (individuals or situations). They continuously look for Rescuers to address their problems for them. Their condition is not their fault, and they don't believe they can change it. If the "Victim" continues to remain within this victimized state, it will prevent them from making changes, resolving issues, or experiencing any satisfaction or success.

2) Rescuer – "Let me help you"

(Rescuer saves others before saving themselves)

A Rescuer in the Drama Triangle feels guilty for being a passive witness to distressed people. They may have all good intentions, and they intervene to try and help Victims but, unfortunately, this practice can give the Victims a false sense of empowerment and keep them dependent and powerless. This leaves them feeling overwhelmed, pressured, and exhausted due to a lack of time for their tasks. They are too busy solving other people's problems to attend to their own.

3) Persecutor – "It's all your fault"

(They are good at finding other's faults and mistakes)

Persecutors blame the Victims and criticize the behavior of Rescuers without providing appropriate guidance, assistance, or a solution to the problem. Persecutors feel they are perfect and everything around them is imperfect. This attitude indicates an "Elite Person" mindset, where the need to win and control those around them is paramount.

They may gossip, bully or talk excessively about others and lack meaningful relationships. Instead of taking the time to focus on their own life, they stay stuck in the cycle of blaming and criticizing.

Now you know the Drama Triangle. Ask yourself:

· Are you a Victim, Rescuer, or Persecutor?

· Have you observed anyone near you among these three?

Humans often view themselves or are viewed by others in various scenarios. It's crucial to note that in a "mind game", the positions in the Drama Triangle can be switched, meaning if one person changes roles, the other two will also shift.

For a long time, the only way to manage the "feared" Drama Triangle was to be cognizant of it and use self-control to decide the roles to be taken.

17. Be Mindful and Listen to Your Inner Child

"Every step taken in mindfulness brings us one step closer to healing ourselves and the planet." -Thich Nhat Nanh

The practice of mindfulness is essential in the healing journey. Practice mindfulness so you can listen to your inner child. When we practice it, every cell in our body contains an awakened wisdom, and that energy will embrace and heal the wounded child in us.

If you are mindful, you will hear your inner child's voice calling for help.

With practice, we come to recognize that our wounded inner child is not merely part of us but is part of a more significant history that we can explore and better understand.

In some cases, our wounded child represents several generations. There is the possibility that our mother has suffered throughout her life. We do not know what our father went through, and there may have been a wound in our parents that they could not heal.

We break the generational cycle of unhealed childhoods by embracing our wounded inner child. We care for our own, the generations before us, and those who will come after. Our ancestors may not have understood how to nurture and care for their inner child, so they passed on their hurt. Through our practice, we can break this chain and bring healing.

"It may not be started with you, but it can end from you."

Healing our inner child can bring liberation for ourselves and those who have hurt or abused us. The abuser may have gone through similar trauma themselves. Through dedicating time to our inner child, many have noticed a reduction in their pain and experienced a profound transformation.

The people in our family and friends circle may also have severely wounded child issues. But if we take care of our inner child well, we can help others. Compassion helps us relate to others and understand them better.

18. Practice Deep Relaxation

"The child I was is just one breath away from me." ~ Sheniz Janmohamed

Deep relaxation is a crucial element to healing unworthiness when using meditation techniques.

When you're deeply relaxed, the subconscious mind will open up.

Once those emotions are exposed, they can be safely and effortlessly released using numerous healing techniques. If you believe that past trauma is causing or contributing to your anxiety, and you think meditation may be the key to help in your healing, it is essential to start with the first step: deep relaxation.

The first thing to understand is that going into a deeply relaxed state is a learned skill. So, like anything else worth learning, it takes practice, commitment, and discipline.

Learning to enter a meditative state

How often should I meditate? If you're starting out, I recommend at least one time a day. Start your day and end your night with the most convenient times for taking care of yourself: first thing in the morning and just before bed. Enjoy a few moments of peace, quiet, and relaxation each day to help you stay refreshed and energized.

If you are a beginner to meditation, start with something other than 1 or 2 hours a day. Don't make it difficult; keep it simple and easy to do.

Also, if you're starting out, I suggest using guided meditation audio or video, such as the meditations in this course. It's much easier when someone shows you through the process.

Part 2: ACCEPTANCE

19. Embrace Your Wounded Inner child

"I believe that this neglected wounded inner child of the past is the major source of human misery." ~John Bradshaw

When we observe our wounded inner child patterns, we tend to be judgmental or blame others instead of facing them instead of confronting them. We try to escape.

Exploring the depths of our unconscious is something we are unable to do, thus leading us to blame external factors for our suffering. Without understanding the source of our pain, we may blamc external sources and continue to suffer.

Our inner child has been hurt badly, begging for our attention and affection to be in a safe and nurturing atmosphere. We are too afraid to feel the memory of past pain and hurt again, and we turn our back. But avoidance is not the answer as the child needs us to create a safe and loving home.

To avoid the pain, we distract ourselves with activities like watching TV or films, socializing, or relying on substances like drugs or alcohol. We create a raucous around us so we cannot hear the persistent cries from our inner child because facing the suffering again is something we would not do.

Running from our wounded inner child only provides a temporary solution- we cannot ignore it forever. We must recognize that true fulfillment and joy only come when we take the time to heal our inner child issues. We must do this to reach our highest potential and truly shine like a star. If we take the necessary steps to address these issues, our dreams will remain within reach, and our lives will remain complete.

Sometimes our issues and sufferings have been handed to us as part of our heritage. To heal ourselves, we may have to suffer a bit. But if we do not heal, we will suffer even more. So, the choice is ours.

While treating a physical wound, when the doctor stitches our wound or puts on medicine, we feel pain and then suffer. Still, we know once we are healed, it will be much better if we avoided that temporary pain of suffering. We think we don't want to treat it because we don't want to feel it.

Do you know what happens?

The wound can become worse and spread a lot in your body. Recalling my father's first heart attack, his doctor advised him to undergo heart surgery. He was fearful and kept deferring the surgery, saying first he would do it in summer and when summer arrived, he would delay it until winter. Despite hearing from someone who had experienced the same procedure, he found it difficult to accept reality. We were hoping he would have his heart operation soon, but he kept delaying it until one day, we lost him.

We often fail to recognize the potential consequences of not facing our fears and insecurity, no matter how much pain or suffering we may endure in the process of healing our emotional wounds. Acknowledging the need to heal is the first step toward recovery.

When we acknowledge the hurt and pain of our inner child, we open ourselves to a deep level of self-compassion. Through this process of self-acceptance and self-love, we cultivate an energy of mindfulness. With this awareness, we can begin healing and nurturing our wounded child.

20. Acknowledge Your Suppressed Emotions

"One of the most healing things you can do is recognize where in your life you are your own poison". ~Steve Maraboli

Growing up in an unhealthy environment can lead to many suppressed emotions, from sadness and anger to fear and guilt. As emotions are forms of energy, they find ways to be expressed, and if there's nobody to talk to, it can be even more challenging. The longer these emotions are repressed, the more intense they become.

The intense emotions that remain suppressed can be damaging. I call this "original pain," as they are unresolved and unvoiced. Nevertheless, we can still access the free spirit of our childhood, which is full of emotion, sensitivity, joy, imagination, and creativity.

Our inner child may be hidden if we pretend, we are happy and healthy, even when we are not. Even if you have masked or suppressed the inner child.

How we suppress our emotions

First: Humans are meant to expand and relish life fully. Our sentiments like distress, envy, rage, elation, pleasure, satisfaction, unworthiness, and so on are all integral parts of the human experience. It is natural to feel emotions, but the difficulty comes when we repress unpleasant experiences.

Second: Unrecognized emotions can be pushed into our subconscious without awareness or control. This process is known as "stuffing your feelings". It can be dangerous, as these emotions can resurface and impact us anytime.

Third: When suppressed emotions remain trapped in the subconscious, they can create a repeated cycle of pain. Deep-seated emotions from the past must be fully expressed, or they can linger and manifest in uncomfortable situations. These emotions must be allowed to fully live out their life cycle to keep from being stuck in this pattern.

For those dealing with unworthiness, this can manifest in various ways and continually resurface, preventing progress in relationships, work, and other aspects of life. It is essential to recognize and confront these feelings to break the cycle.

Fourth: We all have emotions that stem from experiences, even if those experiences happened long ago and in difficult or abusive situations. But the emotions we feel now are ours, and ours alone. It may seem unfair, but that's how it is for everyone. These emotions are not about the person who hurt us, as they may not even remember it.

It's our responsibility to heal ourselves and not keep these emotions suppressed. Doing so only causes us more pain due to someone else's mistake or behavior. People who trigger our unresolved emotions only aid our personal drama; they are our creations and experiences.

21. Silenced by Pain: My Struggle When I Couldn't Speak for Myself

"Staying silent is like a slow growing cancer to the soul and a trait of a true coward. There is nothing intelligent about not standing up for yourself. You may not win every battle. However, everyone will at least know what you stood for- YOU." ~Shannon L. Alder

Suppressed emotions create original pain

I was around ten years old. Our relative passed away, and my mother took me to their house for a few days. Every day they used to buy milk from some dairy near the relative's house.

One day I went with the older person in the house to buy the milk. Next day, someone asked if I remembered the way and if I could go alone and bring milk from that house. Since it was not too far, I said "yes." I took a container and went to buy milk from that dairy.

When I reached the place, there was the owner of the house. He was almost 65 years old man. I handed him the container and requested the milk. That old man called me inside a room, and I went like an innocent little kid.

Suddenly, that old man grabbed, hugged, and forcefully kissed me. I was frozen due to the shock of what had just happened. Since I got scared, he tried to offer me money to buy toffee and chocolate. I felt so disgusted by the incident.

I said no to money, but I took the milk. I was in shock, frozen. My mind was blank.

While coming back, holding the milk container in my hands, my body became so heavy, as if I were walking with lots of weight. That was the heaviest walk I have ever taken.

I detached myself from the present as I could not overcome the incident. It was like I had entered another world where I was alone. I returned and could not tell anyone what had happened to me at the dairy.

The memory of that incident started haunting me almost every day. I was in my inner world, surrounded by emotions of horror, anger, fear, and disgust.

My mother and I did not use to share much with each other, and I always felt a huge communication gap between us. I thought we were in another world while living under the same roof, and I never touched her presence. My mother was in her own world, and I was in mine, struggling with horrible thoughts.

That was the first time I felt so lonely in my life, and I could not share it with anyone, so I suppressed my emotions.

The smell of that old man was coming from me. I just hated myself. Thoughts were haunting me: if they asked me tomorrow to bring milk and could I say no. As time passed, the pressure was building, as I didn't want to go to that dairy again. But what if they ask me why I am not going? What would I say then? What if my mother scolded me and sent me again to bring the milk. What if I couldn't say "no" to anyone.

Since I couldn't come up with a reason to say no, I said I didn't want to stay at my relative's place. I pleaded, "please, Mom, let's go home. But she didn't listen to me.

It was like I was begging in front of my mother, and my own mother did not understand or help me. I felt so much pain, and it was so real and intense. Tears started rolling down my cheeks. I began throwing tantrums to express my emotions as I could not describe the reasons for not staying. I started crying and yelling at my mother.

As everyone arrived at that house to mourn, my mother thought I was crying due to the sorrowful atmosphere But I was scared and was not able to sleep at night. I started crying daily for 2-3 days in front of my mother and forced her to go home. Since my mother couldn't leave the place, she sent me to her cousin sister's house in the same town. She left me at their house for a few days and told my aunt I was afraid because everyone was crying there. I still couldn't tell anyone anything.

While growing up, I started having trust issues with boys. I never made boys my friends or spoke to any boy until I entered college.

I was a 21 year old, a young and beautiful college girl. While everyone used to talk to their lovers on the phone. I used to feel bad about myself, thinking something was wrong with me. I remember crying on Valentine's Day and thinking, why do I not have anyone in my life?

I used to believe that all the boys would start by talking and eventually do something I would not be comfortable with.

I started sitting at the back of the classroom. I used to feel so bad about myself that I began to develop self-esteem issues and self-doubts. Am I not good-looking or attractive enough to have someone in my life? But I closed all the doors because of my fears and insecurities because of my childhood experiences.

I had not found true love in my life, and I struggled a lot whenever it came to trusting people.

When my old limiting beliefs were shattered, I opened the door to new possibilities. Life is filled with surprises, and when I let go of what I once thought accurate, I can explore uncharted paths and discover the beauty of the unknown.

With an open mind, I took a brave step into the unknown, trusting that a world of possibilities awaited me. I embrace the unknown with excitement and anticipation, ready to discover what amazing future adventures hold.

I finally met a boy who became my friend during my college internship. He was so interested in my life and talking to me, and we shared a good bond. I started developing trust on him. He never tried speaking to me inappropriately and respected my boundaries. With his decent nature, he touched my soul.

After eight years of friendship, when we finally thought of marrying, no one was ready in my house. He was from a different caste/religion, and no one in my house was prepared to marry me to him. I tried to maintain calm and convince my family; they tried to manipulate me, but I was confident in my decision.

I was getting so much power from inside to fight anyone who would come between this marriage. I finally convinced everyone, and today I am happily married to the same person. Now, I look back at that girl who was always shy, suppressed, and fearful. How did I convince my entire family of our marriage?

From where was that power coming?

When I tried to connect the dots, I felt my inner child supported me and gave me so much power because my wounded inner child had been looking for pure love for many years.

I feel whatever happened to me in my childhood made me so powerful, and healing made me so strong that I stood up for myself and my decision against my whole family. Today I feel so proud of that one big decision I took for myself and my inner child.

22. The Wound Compound Effect

"Your heart is the beacon. Your heart is the storm. Dare to embrace it; you'll never be torn." ~Vanna Bonta

Misconceptions: With a sad sigh, it can be said that an emotional wound will heal best when left alone. Time is the best healer, and the damage will heal over time.

Reality: Saddened to say neglecting an emotional wound slows down the healing process and may lead to additional emotional damage or cancer. Symptoms of emotional pain can be heart-breaking: hate, anger, stress, fatigue, sadness, irritability, moodiness, resentment, bitterness, manipulation, regret, guilt, loneliness, Jealousy, and insecurity – all leading to an overwhelming sense of sadness.

23. The Walls of Fear

I had schooling at a regular Hindi medium state board school. It was the month of March 2007, and I was attempting my 10th-grade science exam. It was freezing, and the state government conducted the exam for all the schools in one typical government school. (Just for your information, the government school had the worst infrastructure.)

So, the invigilators rang the bell, the question paper and exam sheet were distributed, and I started writing the exam. My hands were shaking because of the cold breeze. I began to feel like going to the washroom to pee. I tried to control it, but because of so much cold, I could not bear the pressure, and I asked permission from the exam conductor to go to the washroom.

But when I reached it, the washroom walls were very short and slightly broken since it was an old government school. Many people were standing at the washroom walls to pass cheat sheets to their friends and relatives attempting the exam. Since I could not ask them to move away, I came back, trying to bear the pressure on my bladder and resumed writing the exam somehow.

But it was getting worse, and it became tough to continue writing the exam. I wrote whatever I could and left my exam. I came home to pee. I cried a lot in front of my father while explaining the whole story.

He started giving me examples, saying that girls these days have a lot of confidence, so why could you not tell the examiner you wanted to go washrrom. He would have arranged something for you. And when my result came, I scored good marks in all the subjects, but I failed my science exam, my first big failure.

I remember one night on the terrace, staring at the sky, recalling the exam incident. I was looking up, crying, and questioning God and the universe. Why did you make me like this such that I could not even speak to go to the washroom.

24. Find Out If Your Inner Child is Wounded: Take this Simple Test

"Your inner child still needs to be loved in order to heal the complete self." ~Karen A. Baquiran

As an adult, you must be aware of specific traits that indicate your inner child is damaged. Low self-esteem, emotional imbalances, rigid or overly weak boundaries, eating disorders, comfort eating, fluctuating moods, or a poor body image can be signs of underlying issues that should not be overlooked. Sadly, these indicators can often be ignored, yet they can seriously impact our mental and physical well-being.

You may feel that your life is fake and you are pretending to be happy when something is eating away at you. You may try to hide these feelings or find that you cannot commit to projects because something stops you. These are again indicative of the inner child.

Put a tick mark on "Yes" and "No" accordingly.

Participate in the test below and tick if you have any of these patterns. [Yes/No]

- I often feel frustrated or irritated. [Yes/No]
- I have low self-esteem. [Yes/No]
- I'm rigid and perfectionistic. [Yes/No]
- I need help starting or finishing things. [Yes/No]
- I give significant reactions when my needs are unmet. [Yes/No]
- I feel guilty standing up for myself. [Yes/No]

- I am not good enough as a man or woman. [Yes/No]
- I hold things and bad memories and have trouble letting go. [Yes/No]
- I am an addict or have been addicted to something. [Yes/No]
- Being overly competitive. [Yes/No]
- Complain that no one understands you or you don't feel heard. [Yes/No]
- I like to steal other's things. [Yes/No]
- I believe I'm a terrible sinner and afraid of going to hell. [Yes/No]
- Difficulty explaining your feelings or why you're upset (alexithymia). [Yes/No]
- I rarely get angry, but when I do, I become rageful. [Yes/No]
- I often feel I pressured to have sex when I don't actually want to do it. [Yes/No]
- I never felt the love of my mother and/or father. [Yes/No]
- A solid drive to achieve constantly to prevent feeling empty or unworthy. [Yes/No]
- I'm highly motivated to strive for excellence and be a top-performing super-achiever.[Yes/No]
- I find myself spending too much time looking at pornography. [Yes/No]
- I have patterns of self-sabotage. [Yes/No]
- Inability to forge strong friendships. [Yes/No]
- I feel more responsible for others than for myself. [Yes/No]
- I feel more alive when I'm in conflict with other people. [Yes/No]

- I'm ashamed of expressing strong emotions such as sadness or anger. [Yes/No]
- I often lie and don't make my promise. [Yes/No]
- I feel uncomfortable and ashamed of my bodily functions (e.g., pee, poo). [Yes/No]
- I am immature or over-mature. [Yes/No]
- I try to manipulate others. [Yes/No]
- Childish outbursts, like throwing tantrums or saying things you don't mean. [Yes/No]
- I constantly criticize myself for being inadequate/unworthy. [Yes/No]
- I don't like my genital parts. [Yes/No]
- I feel so alone inside. [Yes/No]
- A particularly harsh inner critic. [Yes/No]
- I always need someone around me. [Yes/No]
- Fear of abandonment or commitment issues. [Yes/No]
- Recurrent traumatic memories of childhood experiences that made you feel highly anxious, ashamed, or neglected. [Yes/No]
- There is an absence of childhood memories of feeling loved, cared for, and cared for. [Yes/No]
- Current difficulties with anxiety or depression. [Yes/No]
- Relationship difficulties that prevent you from enjoying harmonious relationships or finding a trustworthy romantic partner. [Yes/No]
- Trying very hard to please other people and finding it almost impossible to say no. [Yes/No]
- Feeling that there's something terribly wrong with me. [Yes/No]
- I distrust everyone, including myself. [Yes/No]

- I always experience anxiety whenever thinking about doing something new. [Yes/No]
- I avoid conflict at every chance possible. [Yes/No]
- My greatest fear is being abandoned – and it's something that I'm constantly struggling with. [Yes/No]
- I always say yes when I want to say yes or no [Yes/No]
- I am afraid of some people and tend to avoid them. [Yes/No]

5- If you get more than 5 yes, you should start working on your inner child issues

10- if you have more than 10, prioritize your healing process.

15 - if you have more than 15, please find an inner child healer near you and heal your issues without delay.

Part 3: ACTIONS

25. Heal Your Wounded Inner Child

"Nothing happens until something moves."
~Albert Einstein

Once you have awareness and acceptance, you are ready to take some meaningful actions toward your healing journey. The process of healing has four phases: Realization, Feeling, Forgiveness, and Change.

Acknowledging our role in our pain is a complex but necessary step to healing. As we fully confront the hurt and sorrow of the events, we can start to forgive ourselves, paving the way for us to forgive others. This painful process brings insight and clarity to make the correct choices and to bring about a profound transformation in our understanding.

- ***Realization***

On my healing journey, I have tried to forgive the person who hurt me. I discovered so much more when I went deep down in the process. I understand that two people are involved in the story, and I am one of them. More than forgiving another person, I have to forgive myself for my role in the trauma. It feels like a glowing bulb on our heads when you realize all these years. I regret punishing myself by keeping all my anger and hatred for others inside and feeling the pain and bitterness for all these years.

- ***Feeling the pain***

It is a real pain we realize when we cannot forgive ourselves. Pain can keep us awake for a number of nights and repeatedly remind us of that same pain. Living with that pain for a long time can significantly impact physical or mental health.

One day I was teaching my younger brother, a special kid. He had some difficulties learning and understanding things, and I was putting considerable effort into making him know in the easiest ways.

But I realized that he was not paying attention, and whenever I started to explain, his facial expression became lost, as if he was thinking of something else. I was worried about his future. I tried a few times, but when he needed help understanding. I slapped him and then explained again. He again did not answer, and I hit him again.

This scene was repeated 5-6 times, and I slapped him 5-6 times. Later, I came to my senses and asked myself what was wrong with me. Why have I slapped my brother so much? After, I regretted it a lot, wondering why I could not understand his difficulties and challenges. How can I forget he is a differently abled child?

After a few years, one day, when I suddenly remembered that incident, tears started rolling down my cheeks. Still, while I am writing of this memory. I feel sorrowful and sorry for my behavior that day and for the pain I gave him.

I forgave myself. I am still determining about my brother, though, As the past has no hold on me anymore. I forgave myself at more profound levels through various forgiving practices. A few issues got resolved, few are works in progress. I am healing every day on my healing journey.

Few bad memories faded completely, and few became lighter. I know that day will come soon when all memories of sorrow, hurt, and pain will lose their hold on me, and one day they all will fade away forever, and I will be free.

- ***Forgiveness***

We often say I can never forget the person who hurt us. Whenever we try to forgive, we are reminded of all the pain and hurt they caused, filling us with sadness and rage and making it impossible to ignore.

We feel that not forgiving them is our way of punishing them and retaining our power, but we are inadvertently trapping ourselves in the process. Despite being miles away on a physical level, they remain close, affecting us mentally, whispering in our minds, mocking us, and stealing our peace of mind. Our days and nights are made unbearable as a result. It is a sorrowful realization that until we forgive, we will not be able to free ourselves.

Why are people not able to forgive?

I don't want to forget what they did to me, but I know forgiveness is necessary to move on. They believe if we forgive them, it means letting them back into our lives. However, that's not true. Forgiving doesn't mean we must welcome them with open arms; we can forgive and maintain healthy boundaries. It's the only way to free myself from the drama.

Forgiveness is a powerful tool to help us heal and move on from hurt or trauma. It does not mean we have to let the person who hurt us back into our lives, but instead we can forgive them and let go of our pain.

We should not wait for anyone to ask for our forgiveness. You can write a letter expressing your forgiveness and burn it as a symbolic way of releasing your burden and freeing yourself from the pain. Doing this will leave you feeling much lighter and allow your inner child to heal.

Most people concur that nobody is born a monster since their experiences and circumstances shape them into who they become. You've probably witnessed this yourself: a single family may have one brother who turns to crime while the other goes on to become a police officer or teacher. It's all about the things that happen in our lives, the pain and suffering that shape us into who we are.

In a friendly tone, it's essential to remember that everyone has a unique story, and it's important to be understanding and compassionate.

We are not here to judge how someone has been affected by their experiences. We are all unique, and our capacity to manage our circumstances will differ. Those who inflict harm upon others may have gone through emotional trauma themselves and have been unable to heal from it.

We can try to understand why someone did something to us in light of their pain and childhood struggles. Understanding that these people have endured something that has damaged their inner child can make it easier to comprehend why they can be so cruel. Forgiveness is the only thing that can break this cycle. So, let us be kind and understanding, and let us forgive.

- ***Change***

When you practice forgiveness, you open your door to a brighter future. The opportunities and the brighter future are waiting for you, but you hold yourself with so much pain that you cannot see the new worlds of lots of magical things.

I had spent many nights crying and awake, overwhelmed by the pictures and sounds surrounding me. I was so frustrated that I started talking to myself, as if conversing with them. I realized that I was living in a state of drama, unable to catch a break. But then, I started practicing forgiveness, which made a huge difference.

Suddenly, I woke up one day in a different and better world. I looked for my anger and hate, but they all vanished. It was like they were never here. I couldn't believe how much of a difference forgiving had made.

I searched all the familiar places, trying to evoke the same old images that had once driven me mad and brought me to tears. But they no longer have the same power they once had. Now, I'm in control: I have the remote in my hand, and with a simple flick of a button, I can turn them off. That drama no longer has a hold over me.

26. "Unmet Needs and Desires – The Source of Your Inner Devil!"

"Anger, resentment and jealousy doesn't change the heart of others- It only changes yours." ~Unknown

My unmet needs and desires, suppressed for many years, made me jealous and a manipulator. I remember my father taking me to a barber shop for a haircut, and I told him that I didn't want to cut my hair. I tried to keep my long hair, and he didn't listen to me and ignored my wish to keep long hair.

I cried a lot while the barber was cutting my hair. My father always said, "A boy cut looks very cute on you." He never asked whether I liked it or what I wanted.

He thought I was just a kid and did not know what is right for me. But I did not like it, and no one asked me what did I wanted? Whenever I told him, he simply ignored me. I felt betrayed. I felt not heard and not respected as a child.

For me, long hair = beauty.

I used to get jealous of my friend's long hair. When her mother used to oil her hair and make ponytails, I felt I was not beautiful. One day, I saw her washing her hair with a soap called, "Kesh Nikhar," an old soap brand. I was so jealous of her that I stole soap from their bathroom and washed my hair with "Kesh Nikhar," but I did not like it for some reason.

I did not show her that I was jealous. I used to tell her, "Do you know, short hair looks good, and nowadays, this is a trend." I convinced her by manipulating her to get a haircut like me. We both went to the barber shop, and she told the barber she wanted a haircut like me. She got a haircut and came home, crying after seeing herself in the mirror.

I remember when she bought some beautiful footwear with a fish print on it. They were so colorful, girly, and beautiful. I never had such slippers. I got so jealous of her slippers that I hid one somewhere, and she was not able to find it.

This is what suppressed emotions do. They start giving birth to an evil inside you. Suppressed emotions lead to Jealousy, and Jealousy wakes up the devil inside.

I started taking care of my hair and began decorating it with beads and flowers.

27. How to Connect With Your Inner Child

"By staying open-minded and listening to the needs and desires of your inner child, you open yourself up to the possibilities of anything and everything." -Kim Ha Campbell

Nobody is coming to heal you, so get up.

Tap into the memories of childhood to reconnect with your inner child. Remember the fun and exciting things you used to do during your vacations at home, family trips, or school classes. It's time to revisit those memories with a friendly and welcoming attitude!

Let's have fun today by writing with different colored pens, pencils, and crayons! We all know that playing with colors while painting or writing is enjoyable, so why not try it? Let's have a go and see how it turns out!

Take some pens or pencils of various colors and be creative! Let your inner child come out and explore. Recall your childhood days and enjoy the same enthusiasm that you had as a child. Don't be afraid to doodle on the sides, draw cartoon emojis, or whatever else comes to mind as you answer the questions - have fun!

Questions to channel your inner child

Below are questions you have to answer as a child. Try to write long answers use an extra paper if required.

1) Top three happy memories of your childhood

- ....
- ....
- ....

2) Top three unhappy memories of your childhood.

- ....
- ....
- ....

3) Top three things you loved to do in childhood in your free time or summer vacations. Examples: games, sketching, writing poems and short stories, reading stories, etc.

- ....
- ....
- ....

4) What do you remember being told about yourself by your Mother? Father? Siblings? Relatives? Teacher? Friends? Cousins? (good or bad anything)

Good-
....

....

Bad-
....

....

5) Name five fun things you did with your family member as a child.

- ....
- ....
- ....
- ....
- ....

6) Your three favorite subjects in school

- ....
- ....
- ....

7) You spent more time in your childhood doing what?

- ....
- ....
- ....

8) Who were your three best childhood friends?

- ....
- ....
- ....

9) While I grew up, I always wanted to be...?

- ....

10) What is your favorite season?

- ....

11) How is your perfect day look like?

- ....

First Meeting With Your Inner Child

"I am happy to report that my inner child is still ageless." ~James Broughton

Meeting your inner child for the first time can be a memorable experience! It's been a while since your inner child has been waiting for you to meet, and they have lots of stories, secrets, and messages for you. So why not take the time and meet them friendly and warmly?

Setting up the environment for the meeting:

This process can be so intense and emotional, do not hold your emotions. Feel free to cry. Feel free to laugh. Please keep water and tissue with you in case you need them.

Fragrance: You can use smell if you remember any scent you used to like as an inner child.

Lighting: You can Light an aroma candle or spray some pleasing aroma to bring back the memories

Music: Play soothing instrumental music you feel connected with. Play it on low volume in the background.

Objects: You can keep toys or something related to your childhood in your room.

Place: Use a silent site where no one can disturb you.

Distractions off: Keep the phone aside and switch off all notifications. Instruct your family to don't disturb you for some time. Imagine if you are in deep conversations with your inner child and your mobile starts ringing or someone calls or enters your room. It will break your flow, and you may lose the intimacy/intensity of connection you were able to achieve with your inner child.

The things you will do or say or the emotions that may come out may not be something you wish to share with others. This meeting is extraordinary and personal.

All these preparations are needed to make it comfortable for your inner child to come out. We must talk to our inner child; most importantly, we must let the inner child speak and express in a comfortable and safe environment.

For the things we couldn't speak about because we didn't get a chance to speak up when we were a child, here is our inner child's opportunity to speak up now. Make it easy.

Inviting your inner child:

Try putting two cushions facing each other. Sit on one cushion and keep the other as a placeholder for your inner child. Imagine that your second cushion is your inner child and sitting there. The inner child's age is the same as when it was feeling lonely, sad, and unhappy because of the sufferings it has gone through.

Disclaimer: Don't judge your inner child, be a good listener. Don't judge yourself, and don't worry, nobody is around to judge you too. Trust the process and go with the flow.

Starting the conversation:

You can start your conversation by acknowledging your inner child:

"My dearest [childhood name], I'm here for you. I understand that you have been through so much pain and have felt alone in your struggles. Now I'm here, and I'm here for you now, and I want to be your friend. I'm here to listen, and I'm here to help. You can trust me."

From a friendly place, you can switch seats and sit on the other side. You can either sit or lie down in the lap of your adult self as if you are a child. You can be openly shared and honest with your adult self by expressing your grievances and struggles.

You may complain about how you felt in childhood. Share your pain and fears. Share how you wanted the presence of an adult when you were in trouble or felt lonely and weak.

Keep playing the role of your inner child until some deep unexpressed emotions emerge. If you start feeling emotional and some fearful memories or anecdotes you thought you had forgotten come to the surface, it's a good sign that you're on the right track, and the meeting will be productive and fruitful.

Then get up slowly, go near the other cushion, and say to your inner child.

"Well, thank you, my inner child (or your childhood name), for sharing your pain with me. I am so grateful for your trust in me while you shared your anxieties, worries, and sufferings.

And I want to tell you that

- I love you
- I care for you
- I am always there to support you
- You are not alone
- Now we are friends, and I will keep coming to meet you.
- Feel free to share with me whatever you like or love
- Keep sharing your challenges and struggles with me
- It was lovely meeting you

At the first meeting, try to be friendly and focus on building a connection rather than giving solutions or advice. Find a time to do something your inner child loves. Enjoy the process!

Going forward...

After a few meetings, once you have built a good connection and kept meeting your inner child. You only need to switch cushions once you feel like doing so as an inner child.

You can spend around 15 minutes in nature or doing things your inner child loves to do. Every meeting, you ask what he likes and start nurturing your relationship with your inner child by doing those things. If you talk and listen with so much compassion towards your inner child every day for five or ten minutes, healing will take place, and you will see some good changes in your energy soon and, at times, instantly.

28. Art of Reparenting Your Inner Child

Two steps to start a relationship with your inner child.

ONE: Begin with dialogue and develop a relationship with it.

TWO: Begin to listen to learn more about your inner child's needs, pains, hopes, and dreams, and take steps to make them happen.

Building trust with your inner child is essential. Our job in recovery is to become the loving parents of your inner child. They want to be loved, protected, heard, reassured physically of our love, and guided to grow emotionally into happy and healthy adults.

Who will do those things? To that end, our first job is to daily do something to become trustworthy. We should know what our inner child want from us as their loving parents.

As a friendly reminder, our main objective in recovery is to become trustworthy, loving parents of our inner child. They need to feel our love and be protected, heard, and reassured of our care. We should strive daily to be reliable so that our inner child can grow into a healthy and happy adult. Who else can do those things better than us? So, let's do our best and be their loving parents.

Developing trust with your inner child starts with communicating clearly, respecting them, and being genuine. Honesty, reliability, keeping promises, and being capable are all ways to create a strong bond and build trust. Speak to your inner child in a friendly and caring manner.

Communicate clearly with your inner child

We found a way to survive in our difficult family life - by appearing well-behaved. We learned to mumble, manipulate and say things unrelated to the questions asked of us, or change the subject. We tried our best to steer clear of any issues that could result in us being reprimanded. We said no to anything that could be used as evidence against us. However, in recovery, we learned to express ourselves more clearly and honestly: we mean what we say and say what we mean.

Be Respectful of your inner child.

We can learn to treat ourselves and others with respect in program recovery. We can explore our deep-rooted, unresolved anger and trace it back to its childhood roots to grieve our losses. We also reparent ourselves to ensure our words come from the heart rather than from an unproductive place of disrespect. In this way, we can avoid the consequences of dysfunctional behavior.

Be honest and sincere with your inner child.

Growing up, we often heard parents telling incomplete stories, omitting information, and sometimes even lying. They said one thing but went in a different direction. They cheated and blamed others for their mistakes. Unfortunately, some of us adopted these familial habits. In recovery, however, we confront our feelings of superiority and inferiority. We strive to tell the truth and be consistent in our beliefs, thoughts, words, and actions. Whenever we find ourselves dishonest, we consciously try to stop and analyze our terms and behavior, take responsibility for our mistakes, and practice new behaviors that reflect our true beliefs.

Let's make a commitment to being honest with ourselves and others. Let's work together to create a more trustworthy and reliable future. Let's be friendly and respectful to one another and make every effort to be truthful and genuine.

Be consistent

Growing up, we may have been exposed to inconsistent behaviors from those around us. However, we learn to be consistent in our views and actions in recovery. We strive to use a logical and reasonable process for problem-solving, decision-making, and achieving our goals - all in line with our values. With a friendly attitude, we can be sure our thinking, words, and behavior are always in alignment.

Keep your commitments

While growing up, our promises often needed to be kept. But in recovery, we strive to make sure our inner child and others get fulfilled promises. Before making any promises, we reflect on whether we can make them and why we want to. We consider if we have the time, energy, enthusiasm, and resources to keep the commitment. When we take on a promise, we stay true to our word. In a friendly tone, let's ensure we keep our promises!

Be competent

As children, many of us were often asked to do things we weren't sure how to do. Our parents could have shown us the steps needed to complete the tasks. But in recovery, we become aware of our capabilities and limitations, freely recognizing what we can and can't do.

To ensure we can handle the responsibilities we volunteer for, we might take classes to learn new skills or seek advice from others. Let's be friendly and supportive as we learn and grow together.

"When We Become Trustworthy, We Start Trusting Ourselves More."

As loving and caring parents, we are here to provide love, protection, communication, acceptance, and guidance to our inner children as they grow. We strive to be trustworthy by speaking clearly and reliably, with respect, honesty, sincerity, and consistency. We make sure to keep our promises and are competent in our actions. All of this is done with a friendly tone!

Loving parent talks with their inner child

Roleplay these scenes with another person where one is the loving parent, and the other is the inner child.

1. Introduce yourself to your inner child.

2. Tell your inner child how good you feel to meet him/her.

3. Apologize for hurting your inner child.

4. Tell your inner child how you will change yourself to avoid hurting him/her further.

5. Tell your inner child how you will take care of hurting him/her.

6. Apologies for letting others hurt your inner child.

7. Explain how you will make your own boundaries and stop letting others hurt your inner child further.

8. Tell your inner child how you will protect him/her from allowing others to hurt him/her.

9. Promise respectful, open, and honest communication.

10. Ask your inner child what he/she needs and wants and keep checking his/her requirements.

11. Tell your inner child what you need and want from him/her.

12. Promise you will love, care, protect, listen to, hug, and heal your inner child daily.

Inner children throw tantrums and feel hurt when loving parents break promises. An open dialogue can help us be more productive, fun, and serene. Establishing trust between our loving parents and our inner children is essential for creating a positive, healthy relationship.

To do this, we must have honest and friendly conversations with them. Depending on the age of our inner children, we can discuss various topics. This will help to prevent them from throwing tantrums when loving parents break promises, which can lead to adult procrastination, taking risks, and damaging relationships.

Conversing honestly with our inner children can foster trust and build an effective and loving relationship.

29. Heal With Metta Meditation Metta

What is Metta?

Metta is an ancient Sanskrit word meaning unconditional love and kindness. What should you know about Metta meditation? Metta meditation, also known as loving and kindness meditation, has been around for thousands of years, adapted from the Visuddhimagga (The Path of Purification) by Buddhaghosa, a fifth century C.E. systematization of the Buddha's teachings. Friendly and inviting, Metta meditation is essential for cultivating compassion, connection, and inner peace.

Welcome to the world of Metta meditation! Metta means friendship, and it is derived from the root word Maitri. It is a practice that helps us become friends with ourselves and others. Different cultures around the globe approach this practice differently, but all have the same aim: developing unconditional positivity towards all beings.

So why not try out Metta meditation and make it a part of your life? Imbibe the essence of Metta in every interaction you have with your friends, family, strangers, and even yourself. You will soon notice a magical shift in your life as it gets filled with trust, understanding, love, and care. It's a friendly reminder that we can all benefit from being kinder to ourselves and others.

We are all connected, believe it or not, Through Metta (loving-kindness) meditation, we can send warm, compassionate vibes to others. To begin, we send loving thoughts to ourselves, those we care about, strangers, and even those we don't get along with. Lastly, extend the same feelings of goodwill to all beings across the globe! It's easy to do with a few simple, repeated mantras.

Why not give it a try today? It'll make you – and the world – a whole lot brighter!

We should always remember that taking care of ourselves comes first before we can be truly helpful to others. Otherwise, we may neglect our needs while helping others and regret it later. This approach likely will bring us short-term happiness. So, let's start with Metta's meditation and focus on self-love and self-care. In a friendly tone, let's remember that until we can love and care for ourselves, we won't be able to do a great job of loving and caring for others.

Step 1: Begin the practice with "May I be ..."

- "May I be peaceful, happy, and free in body, mind, and spirit?"
- "May I be free from anger, jealousy, fear, and worries."
- "May I learn to look at myself through the lens of understanding and love?"
- "May I be safe and free from mental or physical injury."
- "May I learn to understand the root of anger, craving, and delusion in myself."
- "May I know how to kindle the fire of joy in myself every day."

- "May I live fresh, solid, and free."
- "May I be free from attachment and distraction."

 Meditation is a form of prayer and a way for our culture to easily experience it. Take a moment to sit quietly. Start sending myself some loving words; for instance, "May I feel love and care," May I have happiness and joy." Using "may" instead of "I am" is more honest and realistic and allows us to make a valid statement about ourselves. Friendly I encourage you to give it a try.

Those who understand love's true essence know its healing power to reduce suffering, promote harmony and bring joy from within. It also gives us the strength to persist in tough times, withstand pain, and have patience until our endeavor rewards us.

Love is like a magical elixir that can penetrate our mind, body, and soul, with visible results in our behavior, words, and attitude. We feel lighter, content, and joyful in both the mind and the spirit.

Step 2: Practicing on others (may he/she/they)

Practice on others, beginning with those close to you. Then, extend your practice to strangers and eventually to someone you may not particularly like but encounter daily. Be friendly and kind throughout!

- "May he/she be joyful, peaceful, and free in body, mind, and spirit."
- "May they be free from anger, jealousy, fear, and worries."
- "May he/she learn to look at me through the lens of understanding and love."

- "May they be safe and free from mental or physical wounds."
- "May he/she learn to understand the root of anger, craving, and delusion in myself."
- "May he/she know how to kindle the fire of joy in me every day."
- "May she live fresh, solid, and free."
- "May they be free from attachment and distraction"

This meditation taught us to be friendly and compassionate toward those who have caused us pain. We learn to have loving kindness and gain the ability to see people's humanity, even if we don't know them. It is also about seeing beyond our pain and recognizing that we all have something in common and can find love for ourselves and others. Ultimately, this meditation helps us love ourselves at the deepest level.

How to practice Metta meditation

Metta meditation is easy and does not require any additional preparatory material to get you started. Another great thing about Metta meditation is that you can do it anytime and anywhere, whether sitting at your office desk, on your balcony, in a quiet corner of your home, etc. However, just ensure one thing till you practice meditation: you should be away from distractions or disturbances.

Metta meditation is an easy and accessible practice requiring no additional materials. You can do it anywhere -at your desk, on your balcony, in a quiet corner of your home. Just make sure to be away from distractions and disturbances while meditating.

Friendly reminder: Metta meditation is accessible and available to anyone!

Step #1: Sit in a comfortable position, close your eyes and take a deep breath slowly through your nose.

Step #2: Focus on how breathing travels through your body.

Step #3: Bring your focus to your heart and keep breathing.

Step #4: Silently recite a positive phrase for yourself. You can say, "May I be free from all the mental or emotional wounds."

Step #5: Repeat the positive affirmations and feel that it is bringing positive shifts within you. If, for some reason, that happens and you start feeling distracted, get your conscience back on track and continue.

Step #6: Begin to feel love and warmth for yourself. Now project that feeling towards those you love, strangers, and then towards your friends. Continue until you feel full of compassion. Visualize and imagine the sensation if it helps. Don't worry if you haven't meditated before. Just try it and you will start to feel the effects! The longer and more intensely you meditate, the more significant the results will be. All in a friendly and encouraging way.

What did Buddha say about this practice?

We all wish for true happiness, not just for ourselves but for everyone else. So let us all cultivate a limitless heart, hoping with our Metta for the entire cosmos. Let's work together for true contentment in a friendly and supportive way.

30. Start Gifting Each Other

"Every step was perfect, like a gift she gave herself, and she smiled, receiving it."
~Madeline Miller, Circe

Gift from adult self to inner child- I gifted my inner child the life she had missed in her childhood, made her happy, and fulfilled her unfulfilled desires.

Do you know what I did to make my inner child happy?

I designed my cupboard to dedicate my childhood memories. There are posters of my childhood which I printed myself.

- My favorite childhood movie: Sholey.
- My Childhood favorite magic serials: Son-Pari, Shaka Laka boom boom, and Alif Laila.
- My Childhood favorite game: Snake and Ladder.
- My favorite candies: Phantom and orange candies.
- My favorite drink: Goli-Soda.

(Photograph of my cupboard)

Gift from inner child to adult self

We have deeply connected and nurtured each other for almost seven years now. Still, whenever I visit my childhood memories, I feel like going to treasure land to hunt some treasure, where lots of glories are hidden. But remember, there will be few enemies in the form of bad experiences and memories.

You can never reach the real gems. If you don't have the courage or don't want to live the painful memories again. But trust me, there is magic and lots of treasures.

Becoming her beloved parent, my inner child. I got lots of gifts from my inner child: courage, confidence, and self-belief, and I got my true authentic nature back. The best gift I got is I found my purpose in life.

I had beautiful experiences while my inner child healing journey.

It was a sunny, bright day when my inner child was waiting for me to gift one treasure box. The box was so beautiful and radiated a golden yellow light. I opened the box, and to my surprise.

Do you know what I found?

"I found the most unique gift from my inner child."

As I opened the treasure box, A bright yellow light shone out. I saw three flashing cards of my childhood memories.

First memory: Opening the first card brought back a beautiful memory of my childhood when I felt hesitant to express to my father how much I wanted a new phone. I was overwhelmed by the thought that I wrote him a letter instead. In the letter, I detailed why I needed a phone, as I had never had one before. Even though we were in the same house, I felt it was the best way to express my feelings and tell my father to consider my request.

Second memory: I opened the second memory card and remembered the day my beloved grandmother passed away. I was filled with grief and sorrow, overwhelmed by emotion as it was the first death I had witnessed up close. The pain was so intense that my emotions overwhelmed me. I couldn't find a way to express them until I wrote a beautiful poem to tell how much I cherished our relationship.

Third memory: Opening the third memory card, I was filled with nostalgia as I had memories of my beloved. I was talking to my love for a month because a foolish promise I had made was heart breaking, and I regretted my decision. I saw myself crying, writing letters cherishing the moments I had spent with him.

Connecting the dots, I realized my love for writing had been with me since childhood. Writing became my outlet for communicating my feelings when I couldn't express my needs, desires, pain, and love. I have chosen writing to express my emotions. And inside the treasure box was a reminder of my strength and capability. What a fantastic gift to receive!

I got beautiful clarity about writing and how my suppressed emotions led me to document everything.

Do you know how much money and time people spend these days just to find clarity and purpose in life?

I gained the confidence and belief to write this book because of my journey of meeting my inner child. I learned about my life purpose and many more secrets because of my inner child healing. So, when you start nurturing your inner child, it will also begin guiding you and encouraging you back. This is a beautiful relationship we share with each other, and we don't need anyone to take care of us.

We are taking care of each other well and happy in our imaginary land where we play, laugh, meet, talk, suggest, love, and demand each other.

"Everyone has unique gifts. Find out yours with inner child healing."

You become strong when you make your weakness your power.

"Turn your wounds into wisdom."

Making our weaknesses our strengths is a great way to become strong. We all have a divine soul within us, and for most of us, it is our life's goal to discover and nurture it. Inner child healing is one way of doing that.

"Heal your inner child and live life fully."

a journey of self-discovery helps us live an authentic life. As we grow, sometimes we forget our true nature due to people, situations, and circumstances. But, if we stay pure, we can keep our soul's true nature alive and reach our life's ultimate goal. Let's remember that our goal is to stay pure until the end, and let's do our best to keep on this journey together in a friendly and supportive way.

It has been a beautiful journey of self-discovery.

Connecting to my inner child and becoming a loving parent had been a fantastic experience. With a friendly and warm presence, my inner child reminded me how far I had come and how much I had accomplished. I was filled with immense love and gratitude for the beautiful present I had received.

31. Is Your Inner Child Healed?

"Happiness is when you love who you are and you are able to accept yourself and others." ~ Bar Refaeli

- **You have more confidence**

Exploring my healing journey has enabled me to confront my long-held insecurities and personal issues. Although I still have some to work on, I am now more confident in speaking up and claiming the space I deserve!

Believe in yourself! Self-acceptance and understanding your unique qualities are vital to feeling confident. You don't need to achieve any particular goal or have a certain amount of money to have confidence - it comes from within. Dig deep and discover the beautiful parts of yourself hidden under your doubts and worries. Unlock your inner spirit and unleash your true potential!

- **You have developed more patience**

My inner child has a strong emotion of anger because of suppression. She has been holding all emotions for too long., and her feelings can sometimes lead to harmful and destructive actions. I'm trying to be understanding and compassionate toward her feelings to provide her an outlet to express her anger healthily.

Gaining insight into my inner child and grasping the link between her experiences and current happenings has given me a greater sense of patience. It's given me the time to take a breath, gather my thoughts and consider the best response. Even if I cannot control my emotions, I can better recognize their roots and why they are so strong.

- **You can recognize your triggers**

Therapy allows us to identify and address triggers, those events or experiences that cause intense and often adverse emotional reactions. We may not even realize that these reactions are linked to memories or backgrounds from our past, but once we start exploring them, we come to see how they are connected.

Without acknowledging these triggers, our reactions can be strong and sometimes overwhelming. But, by recognizing them, we can work through them, process them, and come to terms with them.

By becoming aware of our triggers, we can better understand ourselves and why we feel the way we do. So, let's take a friendly approach to explore them and work towards accepting and processing them.

- **You can soothe yourself**

Self-soothing is a powerful tool for healing that helps us cope with difficult emotions, reduce stress, and improve our overall mental and physical health. It can come in many forms, such as listening to calming music, taking a warm bath, practicing mindful activities like yoga and meditation, or simply enjoying a favorite pastime. No matter how you choose to self-soothe, it is essential to make sure it helps you relax, reduces stress, and encourages a sense of well-being.

We all have our own methods for finding comfort and relief. We might cry, eat, drink, or use substances to feel better. As we start to heal, we may look for healthier ways to soothe ourselves to cope with difficult times.

However, as we heal, the ways we self-soothe may change. Sometimes, crying out is alright, but talking it out with a friend might be better. And you might find that "moving it out" - doing physical activities - can help you focus on your body.

Regardless of our path, healing can help us find healthier ways to calm ourselves and better cope with difficult times.

- **Give yourself grace**

I used to be so harsh on myself, having no mercy for any mistakes I had made, even if they were years ago. I would never give myself a break and was so harsh when I failed or missed a deadline.

But now, I'm more accepting of myself. I'm human, after all, which means I'll make mistakes. Perfection isn't something we can all achieve, and that's okay. I try to be kind and gentle with myself, remembering that I'm doing my absolute best. I try to forgive myself, just like I do with my family and friends, and I also try to show some love to my inner child.

It's all a process, and I'm still working on it, but I'm making progress!

- **Make boundaries**

Growing up in environments where we sacrifice our well-being to please others can be incredibly difficult. We often feel guilty for not giving in to the demands of those we care about, and it can be hard to draw the line and say no when our boundaries are pushed. However, learning to set boundaries and speak up for ourselves is key to protecting our physical and mental health and, ultimately, living a happier and healthier life.

Establishing and maintaining boundaries can be challenging, especially with friends and family to whom we have dedicated much time and energy. Coping with the guilt and sense of violation when someone tries to cross our boundaries can be a challenging experience. Still, by taking a moment to remind ourselves that we are healing and deserve to be respected, we all have the strength, courage, and conviction to stand up for ourselves and create a safe and healthy environment.

No one should have to feel guilty for setting boundaries and protecting themselves since we have the right to do so. Taking care of ourselves is essential to our well-being. By maintaining solid boundaries, We are providing a safe and secure space where we can continue to grow and heal. I'm far from perfect in this, but I'm trying every day.

As I reflect on the 31 years of my life, I am giving myself the space I need to move forward. I am finding ways to remain sane and healthy, even as I set boundaries and prioritize my well-being.

- **You become more loving**

Welcome yourself to the beautiful experience of giving and receiving love. Open your heart and allow yourself to be filled with love and share it with others in a friendly way.

- **You become more compassionate**

When we encounter other people having issues similar to our past selves, let's be kind to them and ourselves. Suffering can bring forth understanding, love, and compassion; these virtues can bring us great happiness. We typically want to avoid suffering but learning how to manage it can be a great teacher and help us become better people.

We can use our suffering to instruct our minds and recognize the value it can bring. So let's be open to learning from our suffering and allow it to be an avenue for understanding, love, and compassion. You open your heart for receiving love and giving love.

- **Your relationship improves**

We try to understand why someone misbehaves or reacts in some particular way to you. Don't just stay on the surface; try to understand the source of their behavior, such as their upbringing, beliefs, and patterns. By being aware of their reactions, you can handle the situation with wisdom and calmness, which may help improve your relationship.

- **You get clarity in life**

Suffering can indeed be a good thing. By going through tough times, we learn how to appreciate the happy moments in life, which can serve as a catalyst to create something beautiful. Without the mud, there would be no lotuses, so we can find peace and joy by having the right attitude toward suffering. So, if you can handle your suffering with a friendly attitude, you won't have to suffer as much, and a beautiful flower of happiness will bloom.

32. 12 Steps Technique to Heal Your Inner Child

(FREE YOURSELF)

"The greatest impurity is ignorance. Free yourself from it. Be pure." ~Gautama Buddha

FREE YOURSELF is a technique I have designed by adding all the necessary steps to heal a wounded inner child.

F- Find out an old photo

R- Reassure and validate your inner child

E- Empathise with the wounded inner child

E- Express with your non-dominant hand

Y- Your inner child beliefs

O- Open up to discovering new beliefs

U- Use art therapy

R- Reparenting your inner child

S- Strengthen your beliefs

E- Exercise with a mirror

L- Letter to your inner child

F- Free yourself

Day-1

F- Find out an old photo

Selecting a photo of your childhood can take you down memory lane, filled with many positive or negative stories and happy or bad memories. Photos capture much more than just a moment-- they provide an entryway to many stories! Even if you don't have a picture, don't worry! Remember any dominating moment when you were younger than twelve and let me guide you through a journey of nostalgia. In a friendly manner, I invite you to go back and explore your past, so you can bring all those special moments back to life.

Visualize your younger self and the memories that come to mind. Take a moment and write down the answers to the below questions.

- What is my age?
- Why I felt those memories are so dear to me?
- Write down a few incidents related to that memory.
- Recall any unhappy incident that happened around this time.
- What were your aspirations at that age?
- How have aspects of your life changed after this age?
- How did you spend your vacations at this age?

Day 1 Assignment

A1. Write down a memory of when you got very angry.

A2. Write down a memory of when you were alone/ hurt/scared.

Day- 2

R- Reassure and love your inner child

Tell your inner child you love and care for him/her in a friendly tone. Praise their spirit and strength and assure them they are safe and secure. Take a photo or other memento of your childhood or visualize yourself as a child younger than 12.

Remind your inner child of how much you value him/her and will always be there to love, protect and understand him/her.

You may also record these affirmations to hear them later whenever you feel low in life:

- I really love you.
- You are the best kid.
- I like you.
- You are awesome.
- You are critical to me.
- I will help you to fulfil your dreams.
- I will protect you.
- I am here for you.
- You are safe with me always.
- I like spending time with you.

Day 2 Assignment

A1. Make a list of ten things that made you happy when you were a child or what you liked to do when you were a child.

A2. Now pick three things that you can do today and do them.

Day 3

E- Empathise with your wounded inner child

Let's take a moment to imagine something today! Research shows that when we use our imagination, our mind starts to treat it as if it were real. Why not use this technique to modify our past memories, incredibly unpleasant ones? Let's get started by writing down and getting started!

Imagine a bad or unhappy memory that made you feel scared and vulnerable, like a scary dog chasing you. Now, get into the shoes of your child-self and try to feel their emotions. Set an alarm clock and give yourself one minute to be in that moment and explore the first feelings or impressions.

Imagine a friend coming to your rescue, a comforting and friendly presence that brings you safely back home. Visualize the feeling of relief and comfort. Allow yourself to really experience that feeling and know that you are safe.

Day 3 Assignment

A1. Imagine a moment in your childhood when you were in a problem, and no one came to help you. Remember all the pain and struggles. Feel how much alone you were. You needed support, but no one came to rescue you.

Now in the same state, imagine your adult self comes like a hero to rescue you. Feel the emotion of happiness and relief. Say thank you to your adult self for saving you.

A2. Write down an incident where you were in trouble, but someone came and helped you get out of it. Write as much detail as possible. Thank the person who rescued you.

Write about an incident where you were able to come out of a problem on your own. Give a pat on your back once you are done writing and appreciate yourself.

Day-4

E- Express with your non-dominant hand

Let's have some fun and do something unique! We'll be communicating with our inner child through writing. Get a notebook and pen, two different colors if you can, and choose a peaceful spot where you won't be disturbed for 30 minutes.

Using your dominant hand, write down five questions you have for your inner child as if you were their parent. Take the other colored pen and answer the questions with your non-dominant hand.

Don't worry about how it looks - just make it legible and let the words flow. Be friendly and encouraging to yourself!

Day 4 Assignment

A1. Describe the feeling in detail when you felt it. Feel free to draw too.

A2. Describe the feeling in detail when you felt very happy/sad. Feel free to draw too.

Day- 5

Y- Your Inner Child's Beliefs

- Write down at least one good thing for which people used to appreciate you.
- Write at least one incident where you felt alone in the crowd or when you felt neglected.
- What was your definition of a good boy (if you are a male) or a good girl (if you are a female) when you were a kid?
- What did you not like about yourself when you were a kid?

Following are a few examples of negative self-beliefs:

- I am weak.
- I am not smart.
- Nobody likes me.
- My parents never loved me.
- I am not beautiful.
- I am too small or too big.
- I am scared all the time.
- I need some clarification all the time.

To know more about your limiting beliefs, you can use the following format:

- "I am strong" or "I'm not weak,"
- "I can overcome" or "I can't give up,"
- "I'm allowed to dream" or "I'm not allowed to quit."

These phrases reflect our power of choice and our ability to create the life we want. We have the power to determine who we are, what we can do, and what we are allowed to do. It's up to us to make the best of our lives.

Now try to distance yourself from your negative beliefs by writing them on paper and burning them. After burning each idea, write an opposite thought on a page one by one. For example, after burning the "I am weak" belief, write "I am powerful" on the page. Feel the shift of thought while you write the positive ones.

Day 5 Assignment

A1. Make a list of things you do not like about yourself that you want to get rid of. Tear the list into many pieces and then burn them to ashes.

A2. Draw a sketch of the person who used to make you feel bad about yourself and said discouraging things. Hold the sketch in front of you and, in a friendly tone, tell the person that now you have grown up and the opposite of what they used to tell you is true. You are strong, confident, and capable.

Day- 6

O- Open up Yourself for Positive Experiences

Strengthen the bond with your childhood and unlock the positive experiences within. Take a moment to sit with your eyes closed and visualize the people who said kind things to you and made you feel good about yourself.

Whether those people were actual relatives or friends or imaginary figures such as parents you wished you had, allow yourself to feel the warmth and connection emanating from them.

Make a list of their positive traits and what they did right. This will help you discover your positive beliefs and boost your self-confidence. You can also think of other adults who were influential in your life, such as a loving grandparent, a kind teacher, or a mentor. Allow yourself to feel the love and security these people gave you and use it to build a stronger bond with your childhood.

Here's a list of positive beliefs that you should nurture within you:

- I am awesome
- My friends and relatives love me
- I am unique
- I am different
- I can have my own opinions

Day 6 Assignment

A1. Write about an incident where you helped someone.

A2. Write about the best compliment you have ever
received.

Day 7

U- Use Art therapy

Art is an incredibly healing activity because it can access our deeper emotions, which are stored on the right side of the brain. This is because language is linked to the left side, while feelings are rooted in the right. With art, we can explore and express our inner emotions in a way that words cannot. So, let's embrace the healing power of art and unlock the parts of our brain that language cannot reach!

Grab a piece of paper and some crayons. Take a few deep breaths while closing your eyes. Visualize the inner child within you, and let your imagination take over. Notice the color of their hair, their posture, the clothing they're wearing, and their demeanor. If the inner child appears to be feeling angry, sad, or frightened, don't judge them. Instead, welcome them and their feelings in their original form.

Using your non-dominant hand, draw a picture of the inner child. Use crayons to color in the areas of the body where the child feels pain and discomfort. Use colors associated with that emotion, such as blue for sadness, yellow for fear, or red for anger.

Day 7 Assignment

A1. Draw a smiling and said face of your inner child.

A2. Draw anything that you feel like drawing using only five colors.

After making the picture, note down why you picked those colors and how you felt while drawing them.

Day 8

R- Reparenting Your Inner Child

Allow yourself to send love and compassion toward your inner child.

Let's comfort your inner child

1. Look at your childhood picture of yourself or visualize your younger self (<12 years) standing in front of you. Try speaking to him/her in a very comforting way.

2. Explain how things were in your childhood home to your wounded inner child. Use specific examples to illustrate the environment you grew up in. Describe the atmosphere of your home, the rules and expectations, and how your parents or guardians interacted with you and each other.

For example, you may say, "Dad never liked me. He always liked my elder brother". You may tell the inner child that it may look like that, but he loves you differently. This may be his way of pushing you to do better. If you remember, he used to scold at brother whenever he could not meet his expectations."

Addressing your wounded child would help in healing the deeper suppressed emotional issues.

3. Unburden your inner child by saying that it was not you. You are not solely responsible for what happened, so stop taking the blame on yourself. Stop punishing yourself.

Day 8 Assignment

A1. Write down instances where things got messed up because of others, but you were blamed for it.

A2. Think of an incident where you took the blame on purpose and felt good about it later. Because you knew that it was not your fault and had no role to play in it.

Day 9

S- Strengthen Your Adult-Self

Raising a child who grows stronger with each passing day requires a resilient parent who can continue to motivate and offer support yet never let them give up and quit. To build strength in your inner child, your grown-up self needs to adopt the role of a resilient parent. Here are some friendly tips to help you while playing this role:

It's okay to make mistakes, as we're all human and have room to learn and grow. As parents, we are responsible for caring for our children and providing them with their basic needs. We must remember that children are weaker, must be protected, and kept safe. Instead of teaching them to please us, we should encourage them to become independent and confident.

Let's help each other out and transform some of our negative beliefs. In a friendly and understanding manner, let's reflect and answer the following questions to help create a positive change.

Why do you think what others are saying about you is true? What are you being blamed for? Was it ultimately your fault? Are you unnecessarily taking the blame on yourself?

Day 9 Assignment

A1. List down at least 1 thing you blame yourself for in detail, with appropriate reasoning using your non-dominant hand.

A2. Now write down as a parent why it was not your (inner child's) fault using your dominant hand.

A3. Now using your non-dominant hand, write down what you would have said if your best friend had made the same mistake.

Day 10

E- Exercising with a mirror

Take a few moments to treat yourself to a self-affirming experience! Grab a large mirror, make sure you can see yourself clearly, and take some time to talk to your reflection. Initially, it may feel strange, but it can do wonders for your inner child. It's a great way to show yourself some love, so go ahead and give it a try!

1. Look at yourself in the mirror and hug yourself. Briefly look at the mirror and embrace yourself.

2. Now shift your perspective and feel that you are hugging your inner child in a very comforting way.

3. Allow your inner child to feel love and compassion.

4. Say a few comforting and encouraging sentences to your inner child, like "I am delighted to be with you today," "You are my best friend," and so on...

Day 10 Assignment

A1. Do the mirror exercise and say words and sentences you always wanted to hear from others (family/friends/teacher/spouse/in-laws).

A2- For the next 21 days, take time to say positive affirmations to yourself. Write down all the names, phrases, and words you wish to hear and practice saying them in a friendly and encouraging manner. Focus on all the good things you want and repeat them to yourself daily.

Day 11

L- Letter to Your Wounded Child

Dear inner child,

I want you to understand how much I love you and how truly proud I am of you. No matter what life throws, I will always be here for you, guiding, protecting, and supporting you through every stage of life. I will always be available for you, and you will never be alone.

The journey of healing your inner child can be difficult, filled with emotional turmoil and memories of sadness, anger, and hate. Please know that I am here for you to help you through these challenging times.

Remember, I'm here for you and love you so much.

Love,

[Your Name]

Day 11 Assignment-

- *A letter from an inner child to your present self,* using a non-dominant hand.
- *A letter from the present self to the inner child,* using your dominant hand.
- Write and respond to each other letters and help each other in the healing journey.

Day12

F- Free yourself

Now that your inner child has healed and feels much lighter and happier, it may want to do certain things. It's now filled with so much more love, a sense of security, and support.

Now is the time to set it free while still being connected. Once you set your inner child free, you will see a boost of the life force within you, as if you have woken up from a deep slumber and have started feeling more energetic and fresher. To set your inner child free, do the following activities without fail. Ensure that this day is a holiday and you have no pending office or house maintenance work.

Stand in front of the mirror, hug yourself and say - "from today, you are free from all your worries" you are free from all the wrong belief people force on you. You are a pure soul, and I love you with all my heart. I will be there to support you through thick and thin. I'll always take care of you and will always make sure that you're safe and secure. You're free to follow your dreams, and I will always support and encourage you. Together, we can make anything possible.

Take out some money, switch hands and keep it in your non-dominant pocket. Pass money to yourself from your dominant hand to the non-dominant hand and keep it on the non-dominant side to ensure it will be remembered.

Go out and buy something for yourself, eat what you like, which you have been missing for a long time. Buy a small gift for yourself. Listen to the songs you liked in your childhood and go to sleep.

Day 12 Assignment

A1. Write down 21 things you are going to do to nurture your inner child in the upcoming days. Promise yourself to take care of your inner child as a loving parent of him/her. Start your inner child healing.

33. Positive Affirmations to Heal Childhood Trauma

"Words are seeds that do more than blow around. They land in our hearts and not the ground. Be careful what you plant and careful what you say. You might have to eat what you planted one day." ~Unknown

How do affirmations work?

You are shaping your reality with every thought, word, and action. Whatever you focus on, you bring into being. So, focus on the fact you desire and manifest it into existence! Your self-talk and internal dialogue are all a stream of affirmations! So remember, you are using affirmations all the time, even if you don't realize it. In a friendly voice, You can manifest your dreams and desires into reality simply by the power of your words and thoughts.

It's time to make a change! Taking control of our thoughts and repeating positive affirmations can create a positive vibration in our subconscious mind, leading to positive life transformations. With a focus on positive thinking, we can even use our minds to heal any health issues we may encounter. Let's start today and commit to focusing on positive thoughts to improve the quality of our lives!'

Affirming yourself is like planting seeds in the soil. If the soil isn't rich, the growth won't be significant. But if you nurture your soil with thoughts that make you feel good, the affirmations will work faster.

Remember that your environment, even before birth, can hugely impact who you become. An unborn baby can hear sounds and feel any stress from the mother. So, take care of yourself and your environment, and you'll surely grow and thrive.

(If you have had a lot of bad experiences in childhood, I highly recommend finding an inner child healer to guide you through the process. They can help you navigate your emotions and provide the support you need to heal.)

Affirmations to love your inner child

- *Today, I focus on my inner happiness.*
- *I am so beautiful.*
- *I am a very pure soul.*
- *I love spending time with myself.*
- *I respect my childlike innocence.*
- *I open my door to new people and new opportunities.*
- *I am improving and growing every day.*
- *I forgive my younger self for all the guilt, shame, and mistakes.*
- *The child in me is free now to explore new things.*
- *I have a lot of compassion for others.*
- *I have lots of love for everyone.*
- *I am a symbol of love and kindness.*

Affirmations to recover your inner child

- *I accept myself in my current situation.*
- *I listen to my inner child's needs carefully.*
- *I trust my inner child.*
- *I am allowed to express pain.*
- *Trusting others and asking for their support is exemplary.*
- *It is okay to think and feel different from others.*
- *Expressing vulnerability is my strength.*
- *I release the feeling of guilt, hurt, and shame.*
- *I reparent my inner child with love, care, understanding, and compassion.*
- *I break the cycle of traumatic thoughts and behaviors that can lead to reliving the trauma.*
- *I am allowed to make mistakes. I forgive myself for all my past mistakes.*
- *My abuse/traumatic experiences do not define who I am.*
- *Boundary setting helps me to create safety within my life.*
- *The people who love me will stay.*
- *I respect myself deeply and treat myself with compassion, kindness, and love.*

Affirmations to nurture your inner child

- *I am happy that I have reconnected with my inner child.*
- *I have a great bond with my inner child.*
- *I fulfill my inner child's unmet needs.*
- *I give myself permission to enjoy, have fun, and play.*
- *It is okay to be playful and silly, even as an adult.*
- *I love being lively and friendly.*
- *Reparenting my inner child has been the most transformative thing I have done for my self-growth.*
- *Reparenting my inner child has been a powerful tool to help me become a more compassionate, understanding, and loving parent to my own children.*

Affirmations to heal your inner child

- *I release all the past pain I've been carrying for years.*
- *I choose to let go of pain and focus on healing all aspects of my inner child.*
- *I am the one who saves myself.*
- *I give myself time and grace to heal my inner child.*
- *I am in a healing space.*
- *I am healing every day.*
- *I am not a victim of history, but I am the creator of my destiny.*
- *It is perfectly safe for me to express joy and celebrate the moments of happiness in my life.*
- *It's okay to laugh and play - it's healthy and safe for me to enjoy the moment!*
- *Every day, I choose to reparent myself.*
- *Expressing both happy and sad emotions is not only safe, but also healthy!*
- *I cherish the unique person I am.*
- *My childhood wounds are healing with every breath.*
- *My past does not define my future.*
- *I quickly set my boundaries in all areas of life.*
- *I stop apologizing for who I am.*
- *My inner child is guiding me and supporting me throughout my life. I honor my inner voice.*
- *I feel blessed to be the person I am today.*
- *My inner child looks up to me for inspiration.*
- *These affirmations are making a massive difference in my life*

- *I am thankful to my inner child, who helped me to become more aligned with my true self.*

Write down or print out all the inner child affirmations you will work with.

Begin by sitting in a comfortable position with a straight back, relaxed shoulders, and a feeling of confidence. To ensure that your energy flows freely, remove any pressure from your spine. Take a deep breath and slowly and confidently say your inner child affirmations, one after another. You can look in the mirror or at the sky.

Close your eyes and focus on your internal child image or use a childhood picture to look at while saying the affirmations. Speak in a friendly tone of voice.

Try to repeat your inner child affirmations two times a day and stay consistent with your practice. Refrain from overwhelming yourself with too many affirmations in one session. With regular exercise, you'll reap the benefits of your inner child affirmations.

Conclusion

Healing happens in layers

"Flowers need time to bloom and so does healing."
~Tina Ashok Dhingra

While writing about my molesting and manipulation story, my husband asked: are you not scared of family, friends, or relatives judging you?

I told him "NO". I promised myself not to suppress my emotions again.

I know there are people who love me truly. They will love me forever. And now, I stopped wasting my time pleasing and making everyone happy.

Today, I am sharing all the stories in this book that made my childhood horrible. They are stories or words suppressed inside me that made me feel hurt, broken, alone, jealous, manipulated, helpless, guilty, angry, less confident, and powerless.

I'm proud of how far I've come on my journey, even though I still have more healing to do to become my most authentic self. There's always another layer to open and uncover, but I'm ready and willing to keep going.

One day while talking to a client while she was sharing her molestation story, I realized why I have gone through all these issues in my life. It is so I can connect, understand and help others to heal.

This is not only a book but a journey of healing. I had tears in my eyes while writing this book. But this time, they are tears of joy and happiness.

I am incredibly grateful for the experiences, both pleasant and challenging, that made me what I am today. These stories are now part of the wider world, and I am deepening my understanding by writing them here.

I'm forever grateful to my inner child for giving me the courage and motivation to write my story. Their imaginative spirit has been a constant source of inspiration and has pushed me to pursue my dreams.

Thank you, inner child, for helping me make this book a reality.

References

- https://www.betterhelp.com/advice/therapy/inner-child-what-is-it-what-happened-to-it-and-how-can-i-fix-it/
- https://www.healthline.com/health/mental-health/inner-child-healing
- 14 Proven Exercises to Heal Your Inner Teenager (+FREE Inner Teenager Healing Worksheets PDF) (ineffableliving.com)https://thebrixtonhousewife.files.wordpress.com/2022/02/656e8-7dayinnerchildjournalingtemplatebyrachelhavekost.pdf
- 25 Positive Affirmations to Heal Childhood Trauma -A Solution B, LLC
- 38 Daily Affirmations For Healing Your Childhood Emotional Neglect (psychcentral.com)https://leadershiptribe.in/blog/the-drama-triangle-explained
- https://www.bethkendall.com/blog/why-the-subconscious-mind-is-ridiculously-powerful
- https://leadershiptribe.in/blog/the-drama-triangle-explained
- Reconciliation: Healing the Inner Child-Book by Thich Nhat Hanh
- Reparenting My Inner Child whose only plea is, "Love me, protect me, hear me, hug me, and heal me." Book by Central Coast ACA Intergroup.
- "The Power of the Possible" Book by Auriela McCarthy

*"This book is a collaboration
between my present self and my
inner child, Tinu, with love."*

www.ingramcontent.com/pod-product-compliance
Lightning Source LLC
Chambersburg PA
CBHW041330120726
48005CB00014B/2184